"What makes *The Leadership Solution* sing louder than most books of its kind is the unending parade of down-to-earth anecdotes, case examples and quotations accumulated throughout Jim Shaffer's five-star, cutting edge consulting career. His unyielding argument that communication drives organizational effectiveness, and thus is the secret ingredient to solving the leadership challenge, is central to the no-nonsense consulting philosophy he's employed in helping top managers of companies across the business spectrum fix problems and realize their full potential."

J. DAVID PINCUS, PH.D
Lead author, *Top Dog*
Former Director of the MBA Program and
Research Professor of Communication,
College of Business Administration, University of Arkansas

"Jim Shaffer shares solid communication wisdom and practical experience for new millenium leaders. If you want to learn how to connect the power of communication to getting business results, read this book."

ED ROBERTSON, Director, Employee Communications
FedEx

"Jim Shaffer knows what makes the future tick. The ideas in this book are invaluable for someone wanting to lead an organization into the future."

ROBERT L. DILENSCHNEIDER, CEO
The Dilenschneider Group

"If you are running a business today—or aspiring to run a business—you should read this book. It's a practical, common sense look at how leaders use communication to solve business problems."

JAMES F. ORR III, Former Chairman and CEO
UNUM Provident Corporation

The Leadership Solution

The Leadership Solution

JIM SHAFFER

MᶜGRAW-HILL

NEW YORK   SAN FRANCISCO   WASHINGTON, D.C.   AUCKLAND   BOGOTÁ
CARACAS   LISBON   LONDON   MADRID   MEXICO CITY   MILAN
MONTREAL   NEW DELHI   SINGAPORE
SYDNEY   TOKYO   TORONTO

Library of Congress Cataloging-in-Publication Data

Shaffer, James C
    The leadership solution / by James C. Shaffer.
      p. cm.
    ISBN 0-07-079063-9
    1. Leadership. I. Title.

    HD57.7 .S474   2000
    658.4'092—dc21   99-087148

McGraw-Hill

A Division of The McGraw·Hill Companies

1 2 3 4 5 6 7 8 9 0   DOC/DOC   0 9 8 7 6 5 4 3 2 1 0

ISBN 0-07-079063-9

This book was set in Times by Lisa Hernandez of Editorial and Production Services. Printed and bound by R. R. Donnelley & Sons Company.

McGraw-Hill books are available at special quantity discounts to use as premiums and sales promotions, or for use in corporate training programs. For more information, please write to the Director of Special Sales, McGraw-Hill, 2 Penn Plaza, New York, NY 10121-2298. Or contact your local bookstore.

 This book is printed on recycled, acid-free paper containing a minimum of 50% recycled de-inked fiber.

Contents

Preface

Who Is This Book For?

This book is for leaders who need to get results by getting everyone in their organizations moving in the same direction and connected to their business strategies.

It's for leaders who understand that all assets are inert until people do something with them and that getting the right people to do the right things at the right times represents a huge source of competitive advantage.

This book is for *Fortune 500* CEOs, leaders of small, fast-growing companies, line managers, work team facilitators, leaders inside not-for-profit organizations, and even government leaders who have the courage to *do* as much as they *say* about improving their organizations. It's for anyone who has leadership responsibility anywhere.

Why Read It?

In an increasingly competitive environment, leaders everywhere are looking for better ways to create competitive advantage. Most know that immense performance improvements are to be had by managing their people better. But many don't know how to do it.

As one broadcasting chief executive once said: "I know precisely what I want to become, and I know our people can deliver more than they do now, but what I *don't* know is precisely what I'm supposed to do at 9 o'clock tomorrow morning that's different than what I did at 9 o'clock today."

This book will help you get more people doing the right things at the right times beginning at 9 o'clock tomorrow morning.

What Will I Get Out of It?

You'll learn how to get higher performance levels by engaging your people in your business, by creating businesses of business people, by giving them the information they need to make the right decisions and to take the right actions, *right* as defined by your business strategy and goals.

You'll learn how to get people to understand and accept why continuing change and improvement is necessary. You'll learn how to focus people on the critical few things that contribute most to your organization's success. You'll learn how to help people understand their role in improving the organization and how they'll benefit when the organization succeeds.

You'll learn how to focus people on working daily to improve the financial scorecard.

This book confronts real business problems. With stories and case studies, it explains how others have successfully negotiated their way through tough issues, such as declining quality and service; the anxiety associated with mergers and acquisitions; downsizing, and restructuring; excessively high costs; escalating turnover and slow response times.

You'll learn ways to assess your own organization's people practices and identify specific techniques for improving performance.

What this book *doesn't* promise is another new fad or "program du jour" guaranteed to deliver instant results. Fads and programs haven't worked; they aren't sustainable. This is a book devoted to hard work, properly focused, which generates real, hardcore business results through people.

How Should I Read It?

The book begins by explaining what happens when people aren't connected to your business strategy and what happens when they are. The point is that from a competitive and financial perspective, you're better off connecting the dots than leaving them unconnected.

In Part 2, I introduce you to communication fundamentals that you need to understand in order to manage the communication process in a way that generates increased performance. I discuss why you should care about this subject in the first place and what we're trying to accomplish by connecting the dots. I introduce you to the concept of engagement—engaging your people in the business of the business. And I introduce you to the components of the communication system, the system that's needed to engage people.

In Part 3, you learn about systems thinking and discover how it applies to managing communication. I'll discuss the importance of managing communication as a system instead of as a collection of activities and events.

In Part 4, we begin to apply what you've covered so far. I've adapted a lot of client work over the years to two situations—a furniture company and an oil company. I've created these situations in hopes that company applications of problems, diagnosis, and solutions will be more instructive and helpful than other formats. And, we'll apply what we've learned to mergers and acquisitions.

Part 5 is entitled Starting Over. It takes you into the life of a business leader who did just that. The business leader I've created here is an amalgamation of several CEOs I've worked with over the years. Confronted with serious business problems and a dissatisfied board, he rejuvenated his company by following the principles and suggestions contained in the book. There's a leadership questionnaire to help you gauge whether you're ready and willing, and there's a list of 20 things you can do right now to begin generating a more engaged team.

Finally, in Part 6, I discuss the communication function and its potential role in helping you manage the communication process. I'll explain why it needs to be reinvented and how you can do it. I'll show you ways to assess whether you're getting high value-to-cost from your communication investments.

This book aims to help you improve business performance. By reading it, you *will* learn a lot about improving the way you manage communication in your organization. But the focus is squarely on performance. Read it from beginning to end. Engage your teammates in the book. Candidly assess your organization's people practices. Begin building a performance improvement plan for your leadership team and for your organization.

Where Did the Ideas Come From?

These ideas came from more than 25 years of hands-on observation and performance improvement efforts in industries from consumer products, technology, transportation, health care, telecommunications, manufacturing, utilities, retail, insurance, and financial services to electronics, energy, food processing, construction, communications, chemicals, government, not-for-profit, and professional services.

They come from years of working with chief executive officers and their leadership teams, marketing directors, product line managers and sales forces, assembly line workers, research and development departments, insurance agents and claims processors, physicians, television anchors, radio deejays, hotel housekeepers, pacemaker designers, greeting card illustrators, communication professionals, telephone linemen, tire installers, truck dispatchers, locomotive engineers and conductors, accountants, mechanical engineers, chemical engineers, electrical engineers, software engineers, preservationists, paper pulp mill employees, gravel makers, filler operators in breweries, poultry eviscerators, and an oxcart driver.

They've come from real-life experiences, some representing huge wins, others representing losses, but all with wonderful lessons learned.

Why Did I Write It?

Work should be fun!

People should come to work each day excited about the prospects of making a difference. They should go home at night feeling as though they did, that they added value and *are* valued.

This doesn't happen enough. Too many people find drudgery in work. Too many people live for Fridays and weekends. Too many people go to work each morning with a lump in their throat and a knot in their stomach. Too many people believe there's nothing to look forward to at work, that work is about putting in time and going home. I've listened to these people, and worked with them.

It shouldn't be this way. Nor does it have to be this way.

I've also listened to a lot of people with some pretty mundane sounding jobs get real passionate about what they do. I know a team of development engineers at a consumer products company who get so engrossed in their work that they regularly have to be told to go home at night lest they burn out their careers at thirty-something. I know a tool-and-die operator at an aircraft assembly plant who comes to work early most days because preshift quiet time gives him a chance to think about better ways to do what he does. I know a warehouse forklift operator who told me the day before Thanksgiving that his wife was thankful for what my team had done in his company. "My work life and home life are better. Frankly, there's some meaning in my life that just wasn't there before we started changing," he told me.

I've learned that organizations don't have to be thought of as places where work gets done. Instead, they can represent gathering places for people to find meaning in what they do by linking the reality of what they do to a higher vision, a vision of greatness for the organization and for themselves.

People in companies that do this have fun.

There's a second reason I've written this book. Many of you asked me to. Many of you who've been clients or in one of my audiences have told me my point of view makes a lot of sense. You've said it's practical, workable, and realistic. You've asked over and over again why I didn't put my thoughts in a book so they could be shared more widely.

So I have.

Jim Shaffer
Annapolis

Introduction

It's like management has this little game. It's called "Connect the Dots." We're supposed to watch what they do, then figure it out for ourselves. We're supposed to connect the dots. What a waste of time and energy. Isn't that what good leadership's all about? Aren't they supposed to connect the dots so we can get on with growing the business?

Dockworker at a trucking company

Y ou can't *not* communicate.

Everything you say and do communicates.

Leaders communicate their priorities by how they use their time, what's first and last on their agenda, who they reward and who they promote. They signal what's important by questions they ask, structure they create, and bureaucracy they eliminate. And when they try to do nothing by hiding behind their office doors, they can send powerful messages that communicate a desire for distance and detachment. Everything a leader says and does communicates something. People who surround that leader search every action or inaction for meaning. And they act accordingly.

An organization's entire systems infrastructure continually spews out messages. All the systems, processes, structures, procedures, and policies send messages about what's important and what's not. Pay systems tell people what gets rewarded. Measurement processes communicate through what they count. The level of resources allocated to an initiative tells us something about the level of that initiative's importance. The amount of structure and bureaucracy an organization puts into place communicate how serious that organization is about cutting costs and getting new products or services to market faster. People in organizations live inside that infrastructure every day. They feel it push and shove, squeeze and release. And they act according to what it tells them to do.

Formal communication channels communicate too. Printed and electronic media pour out readable, viewable information. People study the information, compare it with everything else they see and hear, reconcile differences, search for meaning—and act.

Every minute of every day, leadership behavior, the systems infrastructure, and formal media bombard the organization with an infinite number of data points, cues, and signals, each representing a sliver of raw data that people sort for context, meaning, and direction.

When organizations manage this potential onslaught well, people-energy is focused on successfully implementing the business strategy. When they don't manage it well, people become confused and energy becomes diffused.

Poorly managed communication takes many forms.

Memos may say quality is important, while questions asked in hallway conversation focus on the numbers—quantity.

The president may say customer service is important, but employees recall that the last 15 memos from the president's office dwelled on administrative minutiae, petty policies, and bureaucratic procedures that restricted their ability to serve the customer.

Formal media may say superior performance is valued, but the organization rewards nonperformers and performers alike.

The leadership may preach the need to improve speed-to-market, and then insist on erecting structural and approval processes that fight agility.

Moreover, poorly managed communication manifests itself in many ways. Poor morale caused by feeling jerked around sits at the surface. But underneath morale are fundamental business problems, such as excessive costs, slow response times, poor quality and service, and low productivity.

Communication mismanagement is rampant in business. Employee opinion surveys of excellent and poor-performing organizations consistently rank communication among the top one or two issues that employees say need improvement. Poorly managed communication has prevented many organizations from making prominently publicized "best companies to work for" lists. More than one company has been knocked out of the Malcolm Baldrige National Quality Award competition for this one reason—poor communication with and among employees.

Does poor communication come by design? Yes and no.

On the one hand, no one leading a business today gets up in the morning, looks at himself or herself in the mirror, and says, "Today, I'm going to withhold information from them and see if they can figure it out for themselves. I'm going to try hard to confuse the living daylights out of those people at the office."

Yet many organizations have, in fact, designed communication systems that do just that—withhold information and confuse people. So their organizations are designed to manage information poorly. Unless the communication systems are redesigned, they will continue to withhold and confuse.

Employees represent a ready and welcome group for improving communication management.

Although there may be a few exceptions, people in organizations want to please customers. They want to deliver quality, service, and value. They want to be proud of their organizational affiliation. No one wants to go home at night confused and frustrated. People want to perform well. They want to win, and have fun doing it.

Similarly, customers want quality, service, and value as they define it.

This potential employee-customer marriage is all too often sidetracked by organizational friction in the form of substandard information sharing and mixed messages.

Why?

First, few people who lead businesses today have been taught communication management. Business schools only give it a passing nod.

Second, managing communication is difficult. If it were easy, there probably wouldn't be so many self-help books on the bookshelves designed to help improve communication among spouses or between parents and children. And these are designed to help people within the same family! Why would managing communication among thousands of people from different families, cultures, religions, races, nationalities, and generations not be equally, if not more, difficult? It is.

If it were easy, we'd all be doing it well. Every scintilla of research and anecdotal evidence screams that we're not.

It's tough work. Like everything else in business, it requires knowledge, planning, focus and superb execution.

Connecting the dots isn't what it was when we were children. We'd simply draw lines from one dot to another and a picture would emerge. It was designed to be easy and it was.

Connecting the dots in business is difficult. It means managing an incredibly complex communication system in order to link people's hearts and minds to a greater vision and strategy. That's hard work. Neither this book nor any other will guarantee success at getting the dots connected. I'm confident, however, that what's in this book can work for you because it has worked for many business leaders.

As a passionate sailor, I look for wind to give lift. Similarly, every good business leader is searching for added lift. This book is designed to provide lift.

If you're already a high performer, this book is designed to offer you a large inventory of tips and techniques already being used by other high performers. It can serve as a useful checklist, like checking on your golf swing or tennis form though your game is good.

If you're trying to turn a business around or just entering a major change process, this book could give you a lot of lift—a turbo-boost of sorts. It might help you avoid mistakes others have made, thereby getting you to your goal sooner than others.

Superior execution is up to you.

To close this introduction, I want to leave you with a short anecdote:

One day a man was walking along the beach when he noticed a figure in the distance. As he got closer, he realized the figure was that of a boy picking something up and gently throwing it into the ocean. Approaching the boy, he asked, "What are you doing?"

The youth replied, "Throwing starfish in the ocean. The sun is up and the tide is going out. If I don't throw them in, they'll die."

"Son," the man said, "don't you realize there are miles and miles of beach and hundreds of starfish? You can't possibly make a difference."

After listening politely, the boy bent down, picked up another starfish and threw it into the surf. Then, smiling at the man, he said, "I made a difference for that one."*

I hope this book makes a difference for you.

NOTE: "The Star Thrower" from *The Unexpected Universe*, copyright © 1969 by Loren Eiseley and renewed 1997 by John A Eichman III, reprinted by permission of Harcourt, Inc.

Acknowledgments

A lot of people wrote this book, maybe not literally, but they were right alongside me as I worked day after day at my computer. I hope they're pleased with the results.

Many people have contributed to my thinking about the subject of communication and human interaction. Jack Cudd mentored me in the late 1970s as we built a new communication function at the National Safety Council. Curt Snodgrass, my first Towers Perrin boss, crystallized my thinking about communication as a core business process and the similarities and vast differences between managing external and internal communication.

Rollie Stichweh, now retired from Towers Perrin, has always been an encouragement, as has been John Lynch, who invited my counsel on communication and change issues when he became our firm's CEO.

Over the years, I've learned a lot from many of the firm's best minds on the subject of people performance, but especially, I've learned from Richard Bevan, Peter Bugbee, David Lough, David Rhodes, Karl Price, Margaret Regan, Doug Barile, and Steve Bookbinder. Thank you to the engagement team of Diane Gherson, Monica Oliver, and Doug Friedman, who thought for many long hours about engagement, what it means, and how to get it. Thank you to Towers Perrin's leadership who helped make the book a reality.

Richard Gilbert, over nearly 30 years of sailing together, has helped me understand the similarities between managing a sailboat, managing organizations, and managing life.

Roger D'Aprix has for many years been a very special friend and soul mate. I count his friendship and that of his family as one of my blessings in life.

Nellie Graham, my assistant of 10 years, toiled long and hard to help put this book into your hands. More important, her superb insight into people and her never-ending stream of good ideas over the years have become part of this book's backbone.

Laura Cochran spent many long hours at the word processor, and Ann Finch helped with research.

I owe a special thanks to Paul Wright of Wrightwork, whose strategic guidance, questions, challenges, and refined editor's pen were invaluable.

Spouses and close friends ride the roller coaster ups and downs that accompany book writing. My wife, Anne, didn't realize that "for better or worse" included writing this book. She sacrificed evenings and weekends, especially during the Annapolis sailing season, which in my judgment is the supreme test. She was there beside me during writer's blocks, doubts, fretting, and stewing. Thank you, best friend. Your gentle, caring, smiling, laughing, supporting, loving ways are starting to rub off on me. It's about time.

The Payoff

CHAPTER 1

When the Dots Connect

The root of most conflicts and misunderstandings lies in the absence of communication.

— James L. Barksdale, former CEO of Federal Express, AT&T Wireless Services, and Netscape, now head of the Barksdale Group

First they tell me one thing. Then they tell me something else. When it's time for me to do something, what do I listen to?"

"When I need to decide, I need to decide now—right now. But if I don't have the right information when I need to make my decision, I could make the wrong decision."

"I'm just guessing most of the time."

Confused and uninformed people... they're a drag. They're a drag on productivity. They're a drag on quality and service. They cause costs to rise. They cause everything to move slower while they're trying to figure out what to do.

Confused and uninformed people don't want to be a drag. They'd give up a lot to erase the confusion. They'd much rather be in the know than out of the loop.

They'd like to win over new customers, make customers' problems go away, participate on a team that brings a new product to life, cut new product development time in half, or slash costs that don't add anything to a product's integrity. That's what they'd rather do.

They'd trade confusion for excitement any day. They're like you and me and nearly everyone else. They like winning. They like celebrating. They like to go home at night knowing they did something worthwhile, something of value. We all want to feel valued.

Instead, they're confused and uninformed. They're a drag. They know it, and they don't like it.

In a nationwide study conducted by Bright Enterprises, Inc. for the American Management Association, business leaders estimated that 14 percent of each 40-hour workweek is wasted due to poor communication among employees. This amounts to seven weeks a year.

Confusion and misinformation aren't selective about where they infest a business. Neither is reserved exclusively for the factory floor, the sales team, or all the individual contributors that populate our companies. Leaders of companies can be equally frustrated and uninformed.

"It can be very frustrating," a retail company president told me. "It's like we say it, we say it, and we say it again, and people are just not hearing it. I know it's not their fault. But it's frustrating as hell when we can't connect."

The CEO of a northeast utility told me he feels paranoid about his inability to connect people with his corporate goals. "It's as though some of our employees think I get up in the morning, look myself in the mirror, and commit to confusing the hell out of them. Honestly, I don't. I want them—no, *need* them—to understand where we're going in this new business environment."

"I'll tell you what's frustrating," the head of a telecommunications business unit told me. "My struggle isn't with our 12,000 employees. My struggle is with my top 10. I can't get them on the same page. At our meetings, they sit through the presentations; they nod their heads in agreement. Then they go back to their offices and do as they damned well please. It's like they never sat in that meeting—like they never agreed to a damned thing. Now, how can I get 12,000 employees moving in the same direction if I can't get the top 10 moving in the same direction?"

A recent study by Yankelovich Partners for Hill and Knowlton, a global communication firm, reported: "Employee communication is the single most important issue facing corporate communication today."

Business leaders in every industry are asking the same questions:

- How do we make sure everyone understands—and can connect what they do to—our business strategy and goals?
- How do we help people manage through the constant turmoil of change?
- How do we get people to think and act as if they owned the business?
- How do we engage people, both their hearts and minds, in the process of improving the numbers?
- How can I make sure my leadership is on board, that they walk the talk?

Communication. As the work boss explained to Luke in the film *Cool Hand Luke:* "What we have here is failure to communicate."

Communication. As in, "Oh, that's just a communication problem," or "we're having trouble communicating," or "we're just having a problem with semantics." In many instances, the *communication problem* seems to be something we all accept, something we take for granted—a given. It's like a fog bank on the water. "Guess we'll just have to wait it out; nothing we can do about it," we seem to say.

We seem to accept communication problems because they've always been there, all of our lives. For most of us, the communication problem introduced itself to us in all its glory on the school playground when we tried to get everybody to play the same game or get everyone to line up in the same place to jump rope or play hopscotch, soccer, or softball.

The communication problem never goes away. It's at the office or plant. We see it at home at night when we try to get our friends, neighbors, or families to think or move in a common direction. If you've ever been a member of a homeowner association, you've seen it in spades. Did you ever wonder how it is that two or three people who've lived under the same roof for 15 years could possibly hear the same set of words and attach so many different—and crazy—meanings to what you just said?

Back at work the next morning, the communication problem is …still there. It never lets up. You can't lead a four-person retail shop in an urban strip mall, a 14-person dentist's office, a 400-employee fast-growth high-tech company in Silicon Valley, or General Motors and its nearly 600,000 people sprawled all over the world without encountering it. It's the same problem everywhere. People "don't get along." They're not "on board," "on the same page," or "moving in the same direction."

For too long we've accepted the communication problem. We assume we can't do anything about it.

A lot of people who can't figure out the communication problem, or who feel personally inadequate trying to do so, have gone on the defensive. They start by trivializing the issue, claiming communication is "just the soft stuff." These macho, lean-and-mean, do-it-by-the-numbers chest-beaters quite simply can't manage it, know they can't manage it, and therefore dismiss it. Although they claim it's soft stuff, for them it's really hard.

Dismissing the subject may have worked for them for a while, at least until their competitors began to realize that managing communication well provides a significant competitive advantage and a performance boost.

These business leaders have learned, or knew all along, that creating an environment of openness, teamwork, and trust attracts and keeps the best and brightest people. In a seller's market, people with hot skills can be selective. They'll go where they'll be informed, involved, recognized, rewarded, and respected. They'll leave unhealthy environments of secrecy, mass confusion, and disconnectedness behind.

"It's unrewarding and unnecessary," an employee of a high-tech company in Costa Mesa, California, told me. "Frankly, we simply don't have to put up with it anymore. If you can't lead, get out of the way and let someone in there who can," he said.

Informed people outperform uninformed people, all else being equal. *Fortune* magazine's annual "100 best companies to work for in America" score notably above the norm on communication-related issues. The publicly traded companies on this *Fortune* list consistently deliver higher returns to their shareholders than the S&P 500. Companies, such as Allstate and Sears, have documented the direct correlation between improved communication and improved performance. Analytical rigor aside, it just makes sense that informed people would outperform uninformed people. If you want to win in any field of endeavor, which team would you prefer to lead, the one that knows the rules and what it takes to win or the team that is in the dark?

When today's high-performing business leaders talk about ending the confusion in their organizations, they're not talking about the soft stuff. They're looking for hard returns, hard results, like sales volume, earnings, speed-to-market, productivity, inventory levels, cost of goods sold, and load factors. They're not talking primarily about putting smiles on faces or improving morale. They know that will come. They're interested first and foremost about hard, cold business results that come from informed, passionate people. For these business leaders, the bottom line is the bottom line.

Three different companies' experiences tell the story:

- A quality-obsessed global manufacturer began to experience cost pressures. It decided to relax certain quality standards where the defects were imperceptible to the customer and where they had no effect on product performance. Relaxing these standards would potentially save millions of dollars annually. With no explanation, line managers told employees to not rework the defects out of the products as they had before but instead to ship the products as they came off the line. Over and over again, employees heard managers tell them "Just let it go," or "It can go out like that." No explanation. Employees began to think the company didn't care about quality as it once did. They let other defects slide through to the customer as well. Over time, the company's quality image and sales slipped. A communication assessment that we conducted for the company identified the source of the problem. People didn't understand why they were being asked to ship what they perceived to be defective products. The company immediately explained to its people what its strategy had been and why it had chosen to pursue it. Quality returned to its previous high levels. Today, the company sets the standard for quality in it's industry. However, because it failed to keep its people informed, it suffered sizable losses. Instead of cutting costs through a well-designed plan, it increased costs because it failed to execute its plan well—by not communicating with its people.
- A consumer products company couldn't get new products into the market fast enough. "How do we get our people to come up with new ideas, not just line extensions, but totally new products?" the head of research and development asked me. The root cause of the problem wasn't lack of imagination or an inability to think creatively or apply the company's success formulas. The root cause was poorly managed communication.

No one had told the people in the new product development function that there was a sense of urgency. R&D people didn't have access to the sales force or to the brand managers, who knew customer needs best. The new product development process was slow and bureaucratic, which reinforced in people's minds the impression that the company was in no hurry to speed new products to market. The company identified poorly managed communication as a root cause of underperformance in the new product development area. It then went to work to fix the problem.

- A chemical company had faced a number of years of average performance. Sales and earnings were starting to decline. The president brought his leadership team together and with them crafted a statement of the company's vision, mission, and values. Like all other companies' statements of vision, mission, and values, these read like paeons to motherhood and do-goodism. The president had all the statements framed and distributed throughout the company. The president even gave speeches to employees around the world. Performance failed to improve. Morale declined. "What's going on?" he asked. While a lot of framed statements were being hung on walls, no one was communicating to the people in the organization who had to deliver the goods every day what the framed statements meant. One employee said it best: "I think everyone agrees with all the stuff (the framed statements of vision, mission, and values) on the walls. What no one seems to understand is the *how*. How do we plan to become what it says on the walls? And what does it mean to us?"

People understood the lofty, vague strategy statements. But no one connected the dots between the strategic language and the jobs people did every day.

The failure to explain the rationale for a good business decision, to address communication blockages in getting new products out the door, and to link people and what they do to strategy all undermined these company leaders' attempts to run their businesses well. The basic failure to communicate well. The *communication problem.*

Our research reveals that 30 to 50 percent of employees say they don't understand their organizations' business strategies or what's required for success. A similar percentage tell researchers they don't have the basic information they need to perform their jobs well.

Can you imagine any team in any field of endeavor—sports, entertainment, you name it—expecting to win when only half the team members understand what is needed to succeed? Can you imagine trying to win at any highly competitive game with a team that doesn't have the basic information it needs to perform well?

Aggressive leaders agree it doesn't make sense to go into battle with uninformed people. Some are doing something about it, and they're getting results. Consider these examples:

- In one year, R. R. Donnelley, a giant printing company, realized a $2.25 million improvement in its Allentown, Pennsylvania, operations by opening up communication and introducing small games to improve business literacy.
- In two weeks, employees in one department of a property-casualty insurance firm formed a high-performance involvement team and found ways to save $100,000 annually by managing the company's mail system better.
- A major market television station went from second to first in its market in two years by improving the employee relations climate, as measured by a rigorous employee relations survey, by 55 percent.
- At a major consumer products company, employees came together into high-impact communications teams and helped create and then introduce a highly successful new product line and consolidated costly business systems.

- Within two months, an insurance company improved claims accuracy by 63 percent and reduced claims turnaround time by 47 percent after helping employees better understand how the company made money and then getting them involved in efforts to address key performance issues.

- By improving information sharing and involvement, a food products company reduced turnover costs by $400,000 in *one plant* in a year. Absenteeism was cut by 28 percent and accident frequency by 11 percent. Meanwhile, the quality of two products improved by 17 percent and 23 percent, respectively.

- At a Michigan furniture manufacturer, workers' compensation claims costs declined 85 percent in one year as a result of a comprehensive effort to improve communication about workplace accidents.

- A California utility saved $7 million in one year after implementing a major communication initiative that helped people understand their role in the big picture, provided them with current information they needed to cut costs, and explained how they would benefit when the company succeeded. Meanwhile, the company experienced its highest-ever customer satisfaction scores.

- A major transportation company improved on-time delivery from 40 percent to 70 percent by getting people together to figure out how to serve customers better.

- At a die-cast metal parts company, inventory accuracy rose from 54 percent to 90 percent after opening up the company and sharing more information.

- At a construction company where jobs were coming in 6 percent over budget, sharing financial information and getting people involved in running the business reduced costs and enabled the company to bring jobs in at 2 percent under budget, an 8 percent swing.

- A Fortune 500 manufacturing plant that began implementing open-book management realized the following gains:
  Days lost to accidents went from 50 to zero.
  Lateness and absenteeism declined to an average of one lateness and one day absent per employee per year.
  Returns and allowances were cut almost 50 percent in two years.
  Repair and maintenance costs declined 46 percent in two years.
  The plant went from being a money-loser to making a small profit in one year.

Of course, many factors contributed to these gains, but the central theme for each company was an obsessive focus on open communication, sharing information with people throughout the company so they could perform at higher levels.

Many business leaders understand that the communication problem can be avoided in the first place by managing it well to begin with. Many business leaders also understand that communication is manageable and that the better they manage it, the better they'll perform. But there's another group of business leaders who are still searching for an answer to their performance problems, the ones who ask, "How do I turn confused people into focused people? How do I engage people? How do I connect the dots?"

To link people and what they do to the business strategy and vision requires connecting the dots for people. It means making sure that people understand how they can contribute, that they are able to contribute, that they have the right information when they need it so they can contribute, and that they'll benefit from the results they produce.

Connecting the dots takes time, energy, and work—at first. It also requires a basic understanding of how people decide what they're going to do when given choices. This book is your guide to connecting the dots.

Part One: Lessons Learned

- Communication problems are rampant in companies today. They create confusion and uninformed people. They erode a company's ability to compete.
- It doesn't have to be that way. Many business leaders have discovered that the better they manage communication, the better they perform.
- The payoff has come in hard, cold performance improvements in growth, earnings, quality, service, costs, and speed.
- Managing communication to improve performance requires connecting the dots. It means managing communication to link people and what they do to the organization's business strategy and vision. It means making sure people understand how they can contribute, that they can contribute, that they have the information they need when they need it, and that they will benefit when they produce results.

PART TWO

Ground School: The Six Steps to Connecting People to Strategy

CHAPTER 2

Managing
Decision Moments

*Communication is in the mind of the
recipient. You're just making noise if the
other person doesn't hear you.*

— Jay Sidhu, CEO, Sovereign Bank

C onnecting the dots means linking people and what they do to
the business strategy, vision, and goals. To connect the dots,
communication must be managed in ways that many business leaders haven't thought about.

Usually, when leaders first speak of improving communication in
their organizations, what's in their minds is improving top-down formal communication, such as memos, employee publications, videos,
and the intranet.

Communication is all of this, true. But it's much more.

Communication encompasses technology, telephones and e-mail
messages, conference room presentations, training classes, even hallway discussions.

It includes performance reviews and policies and procedures manuals, safety meetings and breakroom banter.

It includes bulletin boards cluttered with run flow charts and production numbers, as well as financial forecasts and cash flow and income statements. It's paychecks and employees huddled around tables in the employee cafeteria.

It includes video conferences with the CEO and meetings with fist-pounding supervisors.

It's what the work environment tells us is important and what the boss' smirk tells us isn't.

Communication represents all the ways we send, receive, and process information. It's the things we say and the things we don't say. It's what we do and what we don't do. You can't not communicate.

A colleague of mine tried to prove to a group of senior managers at a construction company that you can't not communicate. She explained that we're always giving out signals, that everything we do and don't do communicates something. One bold manager wasn't grasping the concept. Suddenly, he jumped up and said, "I'll show you how not to communicate. Watch this." And he stormed out of the room, slamming the door behind him.

My colleague appreciated his proving her point to the managers who remained in the room.

The CEO of a midwestern furniture manufacturer learned this lesson all too well.

Al prided himself on his openness. Although he wasn't a visible leader, he tried to foster an open communication environment. To demonstrate this priority, he bought one of those red rubber stamps you find in mailrooms with NOT CONFIDENTIAL on the ink side.

As he went through his mail with his secretary every morning, he'd ask her to stamp NOT CONFIDENTIAL on nearly anything of substance. He'd then instruct her to share this mail with people throughout the plant.

But the stamp backfired.

In a meeting I conducted with a group of Al's employees, I was surprised to learn that they thought the place was secretive, that "no one shares anything with us." I probed. One employee spoke for the group. "All we see is the stuff that's marked NOT CONFIDENTIAL. We don't see all the good stuff."

The NOT CONFIDENTIAL stamp's very existence obviously communicated that somewhere in the building was another stamp with CONFIDENTIAL etched on it. But, of course, there wasn't one.

A closed office door communicates different messages to different people. We can hole up in our offices out of everyone's sight, but we're communicating to everyone who knows we're in there. Some people would read the closed door as a desire for privacy, a need to focus on an important task, or a desire to improve productivity by eliminating the distractions caused by open doors. To others, the closed door might communicate that we want to avoid someone or something. It might tell people we don't want to associate with them, that we're too good for them, that we're above them. It could communicate aloofness and coldness, or an unwillingness to answer tough questions or questions for which we're embarrassed to say we have no answers. Many people don't want to be caught not having the answers. Bosses, especially, are supposed to have answers. We don't want people to think—or know—that we're not in a position of power. After all, information is power.

You can't not communicate.

We're all bombarded by tens of thousands of signs, signals, cues, and messages every day. The typical mind processes the bombardment without us having to tell it to. It simply does it. It factors in the sum total of our experience: what we've learned, where we've been, our anxieties, fears, happy moments, sad times, disappointments, and joys. It filters all that through what we really believe, our values and preferences. The mind quickly processes all that information, and then

19

it tells us what to do. On the basis of all those communication cues and signals, we decide. Then we act.

We call a customer. We delay calling a customer.

We answer the mail on our desks. We rearrange the mail on our desks.

We greet a fellow worker with a smile. We let a fellow worker know we'd just as soon be anywhere but here with a casual, "Thank God it's Friday."

We say, "May I take your order?" like we mean it. We say, "May I take your order?" like the customer's an annoyance.

We go out of our way to get a product to a customer in time for her new store opening. We send the product when we get good and ready to send it.

We make sure we do everything by the customer. We make sure we do everything by the book.

We do things in a way that will best serve the customer and the business. We do things any old way.

Each one of these actions follows smack on the heels of a *decision moment*, a period of time when we decide what to do, what action to take. We base our actions on how we process these decision moments. The communication that bombards every corner of the company drives our decision moments.

When communication is managed well, we decide and act in ways that help the business succeed. When communication isn't managed well, we don't.

This happens for every person in the organization, whether there are five or 50,000. Everything we do flows naturally and directly from how well communication has been managed. In turn, the customer feels the vibes and reacts by buying our products and services or someone else's. Figure 2-1 shows what the employee-customer communication chain looks like.

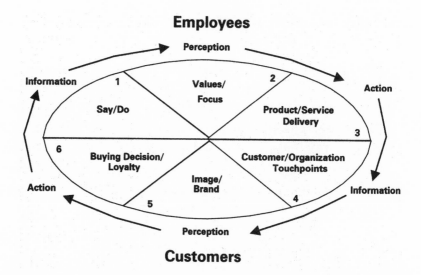

Figure 2-1. The employee-customer communication chain connects people to customers. (Copyright 1998 Towers Perrin.)

In the upper-left segment, segment 1, communication bombards the organization through all the cues, signals, and messages, which come in the form of what's said and what's done.

In the upper-middle segment, segment 2, the communication bombardment creates perceptions in our minds about what's important and what's not: our values, where we should focus our attention and energy, what really matters, among other things. These perceptions drive each decision moment.

In the upper-right segment, segment 3, we act on those perceptions. Our actions create products that work or don't work. Our actions deliver a high or low level of service. They move products to market quickly or slowly. They increase or decrease costs.

In the lower-right segment, segment 4, customers encounter our organization in many different ways. Each encounter represents a *touchpoint*, where customers come into contact with us. They use our products and services. They receive our bills. They drive by our billboards. They talk to our employees in the customer service department. They see how we act. They notice our attitude. They watch us get the job done on time or before we promised. They watch us get the job done two days late.

Segment 5 shows how these touchpoints add up. Customers begin to form opinions about our image, our brand, and us. Our brand represents a promise: reliability; quality; service; low cost; no hassle; user friendliness. Our image and brand are based in large part on the touchpoints that occur between our people and what they do and our customers.

Companies that are good at building their brands know that they're really managing all the things people in the company do to help fulfill the brand promise.

In the lower-left segment, segment 6, increasingly fickle customers make decisions about their future relationship with us. They come back and do more business with us or move on to someone else who offers a better promise or does a better job of delivering on their promise.

The actions that result from decision moments please customers or annoy them, invite them back or divert them to competitors.

These customer decisions determine whether we make money or whether we don't, whether we grow or whether we stagnate, whether our business stays alive or dies.

So whether a customer decides to do business with us is driven in large part by how well we manage the communication that drives our actions.

To connect the dots, we must manage the information bombardment so that we are managing decision moments and the discretionary effort everyone exercises, that is, the actions people choose to take (Figure 2-2). Discretionary effort represents employees' actions

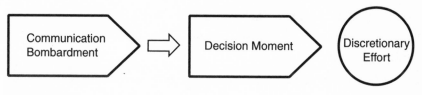

Figure 2-2.

to serve the customer and the business—or not—based on their expe-
rience, information, attitudes, and the messages that bombard them
every day from all directions in the company. How well we manage
decision moments and, in turn, discretionary effort determines our
success or failure.

NASA's Challenger disaster is a prominent illustration of how
decision moments are managed. Engineers at Morton Thiokol repeat-
edly expressed both oral and written concerns over possible O-ring
seal failure before the Challenger explosion. But Thiokol management insisted on a "management decision" rather than an engineering
decision. All the information was available to managers. Their minds
factored in what they thought to be the right engineering decision,
coupled with the risks and rewards associated with proceeding or de-
laying the launch. They processed the bombardment during decision
moments. They pushed to launch. Hard engineering facts and data
didn't necessarily drive how they exercised their discretionary effort.
The need to honor political values and save face communicated loudly
and contributed to their decision—and the action they took.

When we come back from a meeting, we're often confronted
with e-mail, voice mail, and those pink "while you were out" slips.
Sometimes we return the messages in the order they were sent, but
not usually. Sometimes our responses are guided by priorities dictated by circumstances, other information we have available to us, or
by our culture, our organization's values. Does the customer get called

back first? Or do we call the boss back first? Who do we think is more important? What have we told people is important? What have we communicated?

A few years ago, I finished a long day of consulting with a west coast high-tech client. I returned to my hotel and went in search of something to eat. I spotted an attractive outdoor dining area in the hotel where several people were seated at one of the tables. A young host appeared and asked, "May I help you?" I asked for a table and said that I'd like to be seated in the outdoor area. The host politely responded, "We're only serving inside tonight." Appearing somewhat confused, I'm sure, I apologized and said, "I'm sorry, but I saw those people having dinner in the outdoor area and I thought one of the ten or so empty tables might accommodate me."

My host promptly responded, "No, we're not serving out here." He pointed to the occupied table and said, "Those people are different. That's the general manager and his family."

Somebody hadn't connected the dots for this young man. Somewhere, someone at some time had communicated clearly to this poor fellow that the boss was different, certainly different from the customer. Different, to him, meant special. I'm quite sure that no one had ever come right out and said, "Hey buddy, that general manager over there is a lot more important than our customers." But I *would* bet that through a multiplicity of deferential comments and treatment and the general manager's acceptance of deferential comments and treatment, with a little body language thrown in here and there, the aggregate communication to this young host was: "Hey buddy, that general manager over there is a lot more important than our customers." And so, when the employee processed my request for a table in his mind, *during a decision moment*, the little voice inside his head said, "The boss gets the table outside if he wants it, but the customer wanting dinner outside doesn't." The action he took spoke volumes. Confronted with a decision moment, he exercised his awareness of all the information that had bombarded him, formally and informally, over time. He exercised his discretionary effort in a way that devalued my importance as a customer.

An airline I try to avoid (because they consistently reinforce their poor image by the way they treat their customers) but couldn't because they (like many airlines these days) dominate a certain U.S. airport, made a mistake that caused me and several other passengers a major inconvenience. The gate agent admitted the mistake but said he couldn't do anything about it. My fellow inconvenienced passengers and I pointed out what we thought were realistic ways to remedy the problem. None would have cost a dime. He said he was sorry but he didn't have authority to do anything about the problem, including acting on any of our suggestions. This gate agent could have managed his discretionary effort either toward or away from the customer. He managed it away from the customer because somewhere along the line, the airline (undoubtedly, his supervisors and ultimately the airline's leadership) had communicated to him in no uncertain terms that he was to be a slave to the rulebook, not to the customer. He didn't have authority to improve the airline's lousy reputation.

Every day, this airline has thousands of opportunities to manage its employees' decision moments toward their customers and toward reversing their pitiful but well-deserved reputation. But, it has chosen not to do so. Instead, it has chosen to constrict its people, deny them the opportunity to improve the business, and perpetuate its lousy reputation.

Gordon Bethune has taken exactly the opposite approach at Continental Airlines. In five years he has turned the company around—the workforce and the financial statements. Bethune epitomizes the CEO who understands the need to communicate to connect people to the business.

"The time that Bethune spends communicating with and exhorting employees is astounding," Brian O'Reilly wrote in *Fortune* magazine.

When business leaders don't connect the dots for their people, they lose thousands of opportunities to improve their business every day. Yet they sometimes act surprised when the numbers start heading south.

Every time someone invests in a piece of technology, the action arrives after a decision moment. Every time an employee dreams up a new product idea, it comes after a decision moment. Every time someone in an auto manufacturing plant takes the time to eliminate a paint imperfection, that, too, comes after a decision moment.

Shipping a defective product comes after a decision moment. Slighting a customer by saying "I don't know" and making no effort to find out comes after a decision moment. Every time the receptionist at your doctor's office is curt, rude, or unwilling to go the extra mile to help, the action comes after a decision moment.

When we recognize, value, and successfully manage decision moments, people do things that help the business win. The product of decision moments should be actions that contribute to winning.

But none of this will happen if we don't manage the driver of the decision moments, the communication bombardment.

Managing decision moments means connecting people's hearts and minds to the business and what is required for the business to succeed. Never has this been more urgent or more crucial to success than today.

Why? What's changed? In two words, market forces, including mergers, acquisitions, deregulation, globalization, and rapidly evolving technology. The dynamics of today's marketplace have redefined the nature of work and the relationship people have with the organizations they join. We've heard this before, but let's take a few moments to consider the shift that's occurred.

For decades, after the turn of the twentieth century, work was quite different from now. Formal, written job descriptions defined the typical job, which often tended to consist of relatively simple rote procedures. It was easier to hire people who did simple tasks than it was people who performed complex tasks. Because knowledgeable, skilled people were difficult to replace, companies tried to keep work simple. Hiring replacements was a full-time job for many companies that had to hire thousands of people yearly just to replace those who were sick, walked out, quit, or went on strike.

Lines of authority were clearly laid out. The boss made the decisions. It was his job (and it usually was a *him*) to hire people, show them their job, tell them what to do, expect them to do it, pay them, and mete out any necessary discipline. People were told what to do and they were expected to do it. There was little if any discretion in a job. "Don't think about it, just do it," bosses warned.

The prevailing management style was usually autocratic and patriarchal. The prevailing culture was paternalistic. "If you do an honest day's work for an honest day's pay, we'll take care of you." Companies valued loyalty and long service. Organizations often went to great lengths (surprisingly, some still do) to adorn their hallway walls with pictures of people who made the "35-Year Club" and the "40-Year Club," people who had been with the company seemingly forever.

These work practices became ingrained in most organizations' cultures.

Then, rapid-fire business and work environment changes forced companies to reconsider and adapt their approach to managing people.

Technology, of course, abetted by speeding everything up. Technology has enabled everyone to do more, stretching resources far beyond the apparent limits of old. As a result, our expectations as customers have grown. In less than 20 years, we've moved from three-day postal delivery to overnight delivery to fax delivery to real-time online delivery.

Ten years ago, it could take several days or even weeks for an employee to get price information for a customer. Today, anyone with e-mail can pose a question and get an answer from anyone else in the organization, including, in many cases, the CEO.

Along the way, work changed. It has grown less hierarchical and more process-oriented. It often spans traditional functions and is frequently performed in teams. Teams focus on serving customers quickly. People in the field, on the road, or telecommuting from home offices can now operate without supervisors for weeks at a time. An increasing number of companies are building work groups with no designated leader. According to Ed Lawler, head of the University of Southern California's Center for Effective Organizations, less than 30 percent of the largest publicly traded companies had self-directed teams in 1987. Today, that number has risen to nearly 80 percent.[1]

People in today's companies have changed, too. Values are different. A decade of downsizing severed the social contract and created new reciprocal deals between organizations and their people. A need for commitment to good service to the customer has replaced commitment to long service to the organization, because customers now can say, "If you don't deliver what I want, someone else will. I have the flexibility and mobility to go elsewhere."

A generation has grown used to feeling more in control of what they see, hear, and say on the job. They're manipulating buttons, switches, remotes, and mouses. Pay and benefits are important still but only as antes into the game. People expect greater control of and flexibility in their work. They also want an exciting work environment and an opportunity to learn and grow. If they don't get what they want, they'll go elsewhere to a company that meets their needs. Because job security and long service have ceased to be work force values, people will just keep moving until they find the values that matter to them.

In one effort to improve performance a few years ago, some managers began to make some attempts at yielding control. This trend was referred to as *empowerment*. But many managers didn't know what it meant. Some saw it as merely another business fad. Some saw it as a chance to carve away at the bloated bureaucracies they'd created. Some said it meant pushing decision-making down. Some felt threatened because they thought empowerment meant giving up all the control that they had "earned" during their years of moving up the management ranks.

While many companies trundled through the empowerment craze, similar to how they trundled through the quality craze and the reengineering craze, that small group of high performers that almost always do things well grabbed the notion of empowerment and used it successfully to improve performance. They understood that empowerment represents, to use expert Peter Block's words, a "state of mind as well as a result of position, policies, and practices." As Block, author of the mid-eighties best-selling book, *The Empowered Manager*, explained to us: "As managers, we become more powerful as we nurture the power of those below us."

Nurturing that power means sharing vast amounts of information with people so they have what they need to make informed decisions.

"Sharing as much information as possible is the opposite of the military notion that only those who 'need to know' should be informed," Block said. He went on:

> Most supervisors think part of their role is to shield their subordinates from bad news coming from above. When we shield our people, we are acting as their parents and treating them like children. If we are trying to create the mindset that everyone is responsible for the success of this business, then our people need complete information. We need to think of our subordinates and bosses as partners rather than as children or parents. Most of us know that if we withheld information from our partners, we would be putting the relationship at risk.

Many empowerment efforts failed because managers weren't comfortable sharing the vast amounts of information people require before they are genuinely empowered. "People don't understand that you don't just push decisions down simply by telling more people to make more decisions," the chairman of an electric power company in the South told me. "If you do," he went on, "you're just increasing the level of uninformed decision-making."

The empowerment craze may be dead and gone. However, the need to create informed, fast-moving, agile, adaptable, cost-effective teams is still increasing exponentially as we discover daily that these teams represent the key to winning.

To link people to the business and its strategies and goals, to *engage* people, you need to make sure your people have the information prescribed in Figure 2-3.

Engagement has four primary components:

- Line of sight
- Involvement
- Information sharing
- Rewards and recognition

Let's look at each.

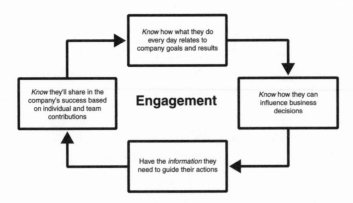

Figure 2-3. Linking people to strategy.

Line of Sight

Line of sight means that people can see a direct line between the organization's goals and what they do.

They understand the big picture. The can connect the dots between what they do and the ultimate impact they have.

Big picture means the high-level financial, market, and strategic aspects of the business. So understanding those things means they know what shareholder value is and what the business drivers are. They understand the company's strategy for creating short- and long-term results. Building line of sight requires intense, ongoing communication.

Imagine being in an airplane's flight deck. Most of us would have absolutely no idea what all those switches, buttons, toggles, and levers do. We would just know that there are a bunch of switches, buttons, toggles, and levers, and that somehow, some way, there's a connection between them and the airplane's movements. Something just happens. We don't have line of sight.

Imagine now that you've just returned from flight school and you understand what every one of those switches, buttons, toggles, and levers does, how each influences the airplane and to what degree. You now understand how they work together to cause the airplane to do what it does. You know when you reach over and pull this particular lever what corresponding impact there will be on the airplane's movements. You now have line of sight.

Do the people in your organization have line of sight? All of them? It's the first step in connecting the dots.

Involvement

Through involvement, people have the means to influence the organization. Involvement encompasses team systems, process redesign efforts, and keeping score together. Involvement includes the means through which people's ideas for improving business results are generated, captured, prioritized, analyzed, and implemented. Involvement also includes the process through which people participate in setting goals and making forecasts.

Involvement is a component of the communication process. Take communication away and no one's involved.

Stepping back into the flight deck, when someone establishes a flight plan and manipulates the switches, buttons, toggles, and levers so the plane rolls down the runway, becomes airborne, flies to its destination, and lands, that person is involved. In a small, single-engine airplane, a solo pilot might do it all. On a passenger jet, roles and responsibilities might be divided up. Involvement includes planning, deciding, and doing.

How involved are your people? How much control do they have over what they do?

Information Sharing

"You can hire the best people in the world. You can train them within an inch of their lives. But if they don't have regular, ongoing access to information, they won't be able to make smart decisions." Those are the words of Pat Kelly, founder and CEO of the hypergrowth company PSS/World Medical, Inc., based in Jacksonville, Florida.

You can understand your goals and how you can influence them, but unless you have a continuous flow of accurate, timely information, you won't have the information you need to make the right decisions when you need to. The dots won't connect. Information *is* power.

Back in the airplane, the pilot needs a continuous flow of information regarding altitude, wind speed, temperature, plane speed, and heading in order to fly the airplane effectively and efficiently.

Because today's businesses are so dynamic, changing from minute to minute, we need to make sure we're providing people throughout our enterprises with the information they need, when they need it, to make the right decisions on behalf of the team. People need information at twitch speed. Twitch speed is fast. Anything less slows decision-making down. And when decision-making slows down, business slows down. In today's competitive world, opportunity follows speed. We can't slow anything down without a cost. Especially information sharing.

Many business leaders who are new to the notion of sharing large amounts of information have shared their skepticism with me. Here's what some of them say, along with my response.

- "I'm afraid to let go." *What you think you have control over is probably an illusion. Withholding information is the equivalent of withholding power. You will be more apt to control the results if you give control to people who can deliver the results.*
- "Our employees might use the information against us. I don't want them giving information out at parties and the local saloon." *There's always going to be information that shouldn't be widely shared. But employees with a stake in the action aren't apt to share information that could be used against them. As you provide more information to people, it's important for them to know that sharing in a partnership constitutes an adult relationship unlike the "need to know" adult-child relationship of the past.*
- "Unions will find out and use it as bargaining leverage." *The point of connecting the dots is to create a partnership of engaged people. If the "deal" you have with your people is fair, well-understood, and accepted, and if you're living up to your end of the deal, there's little that can be held against you by sharing information more widely.*
- "Our customers might find out that our prices are too high." *Or that your value is too low.*

- "Isn't some information in a publicly held business 'material' in the eyes of the U.S. Securities and Exchange Commission?" *Yes. But many publicly held companies that practice open-book management avoid the problem by deliberately omitting some types of information from the information sharing process. These omissions help prevent someone from trading on the information. Some smaller companies make all their employees insiders for purposes of financial disclosure laws. But in general, most companies can afford to share a lot more information than they do now before they'll bump up against financial disclosure laws.*

- "I'm not comfortable giving out bad news." *It's certainly not easy, but the reality is that your people know when things aren't going well. Often, they know before you do. The number of orders they ship declines. Inventory backs up. People aren't as busy. Sales people hear "no" more than usual. Smoking breaks are a little more frequent and last longer. People watch for all the proxies of good and bad news. If you don't share bad news as well as good, good news will become blunted while bad news will be accentuated. If I had a team on the field and they were losing and we only had a few minutes to play, I know I'd tell them so we could pick the game up a little or change what we were doing. If I didn't tell them and we lost, I'd feel I contributed unnecessarily to the loss. That creates victims. People don't want to lose. My experience suggests that you'll be more apt to improve a bad situation with informed people than uninformed people.*

- "Can you really get people to understand a lot of financial information?" *Yes, if you talk to them from their perspective and not from the chief financial officer's perspective (although I know some CFOs who are excellent teachers of business literacy). Remember that these people are the ones who are financing their*

*children's educations, serving as treasurers on civic organiza-
tions, negotiating mortgages, and balancing their own checkbooks. Historically, we've treated them like children and assumed they couldn't understand basic business finance. If we
want adults at work, we need to treat people as adults. Treating
people as adults means, in part, making sure they understand
what they're doing and why. A trip to a company that opens the
books to their people will remove all doubts you've ever had that
people "just won't understand the numbers." Only hubris would
perpetuate the myth that "I can understand it but they can't."*

Do your people—all your people—have all the information they
need—when they need it—to perform at their peak?

Rewards and Recognition

Rewards and recognition answer the questions "What's in it for me?"
and "How will I benefit if I do things that will help our business succeed?" Rewards and recognition include short-term incentives for individuals and teams; broad-based success sharing programs; recognition and celebrations; long-term wealth-building programs, such as
savings and stock programs; and nonfinancial rewards, such as opportunities to learn, paths for career advancement and growth, and the
opportunity to work in an exciting, fun, and cool environment.

Reward and recognition systems are components of the communication process. The mere design of a reward scheme should communicate what's important and what's not. What we choose to recognize communicates what we value.

How well does your reward and recognition system communicate
what you want done? Are you sure?

*Your people will become engaged when you connect the dots. The
dots will connect when we help people understand the big picture, get*

them involved in running the business, provide huge amounts of deci-
sion-making information, and make sure they understand WIIFM—
what's in it for me.

This is what the best of the best do to connect the dots. Let's ex-
plore each of these connectors more.

CHAPTER 3

Guiding by Best Principles

Communication isn't separate from the business; it's the way we do business.

— Larry Bossidy, Chairman, AlliedSignal

Many businesses connect the dots. A lot of organizations manage to get their people on board, connected, engaged, committed, excited, and turned on to what they're doing and where they're going. Some are big companies we've all heard about. Others are little businesses nestled in industrial parks or urban strip malls. They span industries from retail to manufacturing, from financial services to high technology. No industry is either handicapped or advantaged in its attempt to connect the dots. Any organization in any line of business can do it.

Who connects the dots best? Where are they? What are their secrets? What guides them? What can we learn from them?

Many of the companies on *Fortune's* "100 Best Companies to Work for in America" list connect the dots. Having worked with companies that are on the list and wanted to join that list, I can tell you that many of the characteristics that qualify a company for this list are the same as those required to connect the dots. It's sort of like if you can play the trumpet, you can play the cornet. The instruments are nearly identical from the musician's perspective.

Robert Levering and Milton Moskowitz created the 100 Best Companies list. Two thirds of their scoring of companies competing for a slot on the list is based on answers employees give to a 57-question survey. The questions relate to leadership credibility, respect, fairness, pride, and camaraderie. Many of the questions are similar, if not identical, to a survey that would measure engagement or commitment.[*]

These companies are able to attract some of the best and brightest people because they create organizations that people gravitate to. "In an ultratight labor market, companies primp to woo and retain talent," Levering and Moskowitz stated in a *Fortune* article announcing the Year 2000 winners. Because they receive far more applications for employment than they can ever accommodate (the average company on the Year 2000 list has 5125 employees and received 16,289 job applications), they're able to cherry pick the best talent.

Once the best get on board, they perform. Shares of the 58 publicly held companies on the list rose 37 percent annualized over the past three years, compared with 25 percent for the S&P 500. Qualcomm led with a 1500 percent increase in 1999.[2]

Some members on the list are huge. They include Lucent Technologies (118,000 employees), Marriott International (126,000 associates), and Hewlett-Packard (83,000 employees). Some are relatively little, Fenwick & West, a Palo Alto law firm; consultant Scitor, business software maker; Great Plains and Granite Rock, a construction firm, all have less than 1000 people.

Companies that practice open-book management tend to connect the dots well. Open-book management is a leadership philosophy that's grounded in the notion of creating businesses of business people;

*See Chapter 11 for more discussion of The Engagement Index.

everyone in the organization thinks and acts like a business owner. People in pure, open-book companies are steeped in business literacy, work daily to improve the financials, have huge amounts of financial information available to them (hence, the term *open-book*), and their rewards and recognition are tied to financial performance. People are immersed in all four components of engagement—line of sight, involvement, information sharing, and rewards and recognition.

Springfield ReManufacturing Corporation (SRC), located in Springfield, Missouri, is the open-book pioneer. SRC was a branch of International Harvester until the early 1980s, when Harvester announced it would close the branch. Jack Stack, now its president, and 12 other managers bought the company. The terms of the sale left the company with an 89:1 debt-to-equity ratio. Since then, SRC's shareholder return has increased 40,000 percent.

If you visit one of SRC's superb seminars, which describe how they've achieved those returns, you should pay a visit to Johnny out in the factory. Ask him what he does. The only problem with what he'll tell you is that unless you have a pretty fair grasp of business finance and accounting, you'll not catch all of it. Johnny's no financial guy. He cleans out old truck engines. But because he's in an open-book company, his primary job is to help run the business. His other job is to clean out truck engines. Johnny can tell you to within a penny or two how the company's doing against its forecasts on any given day and what he and his colleagues have to do to make plan. Then he'll be glad to tell you exactly—to the penny—what all of that means in terms of his pay, bonus, and profit sharing.

Johnny is not unusual. There are a lot of Johnnys in open-book companies. That's why these companies succeed.

Open-book companies tend to be smaller, fast-growth companies. They're smaller for two reasons.

First, the open-book concept took hold well after the corporate giants got to be giants. Introducing the open-book philosophy to a large company is best done in chunks. It's not something that can be quickly "installed" in a large company. R.R. Donnelley & Sons, the global printing company, introduced open-book management first in one of its plants in its northeastern division in Allentown, Pennsylvania, then spread it to nearby plants within the division. Hexacomb, a division of Tenneco Packaging, and Heflin Steel, an Esco business group, have introduced open-book management concepts, as have divisions or business units of many other large companies.

Second, because it's a relatively new concept, it's been grabbed by hundreds of newer, smaller, but fast-growing companies, such as PSS/World Medical, which since 1987 has been growing at an average rate of 40 percent per year with same-store growth of 22 percent annually, compared to an industry average of 3 percent. Its work force has grown from 120 to 2500 people. Among the other companies that have adopted open-book principles are Patagonia, Southwest Airlines, Amoco Canada, Harley-Davidson, The Body Shop, and Chick-fil-A. Each year, Springfield ReManufacturing sponsors a National Gathering of the Games (which is associated with Stack's Great Game of Business concept of open-book management) where hundreds of people representing open-book companies gather to share war stories, brag about their successes, and learn about ways to improve their businesses.

Today, the term open-book management isn't used as much as it was five or ten years ago. However, the practices of building business literacy, sharing financial information, involving people in decision-making, and tying incentives to performance are more prevalent than ever in traditional companies and especially in the fast startup companies such as the dot coms. It has become a way to run a business today rather than a term.

I've been inside open-book companies, just as I've been inside companies on the *Fortune* best-to-work-for list. I've been inside many of the companies that connect the dots: Microsoft, FedEx, American

Century, Hewlett-Packard, AlliedSignal, SRC, Physician's Sales and Service, Johnson & Johnson, the Bureau of National Affairs, Ingram Micro, Procter & Gamble, Marriott International, UnumProvident, 3M, Medtronic, Herman Miller, Hallmark Cards, Fannie Mae, Motorola, and Toyota. None of them use any special tricks that aren't available to anyone else. There's no "connect-the-dots store" that you can enter with a secret handshake and uncover mysteries unavailable to those who don't know the handshake. None of them have access to any websites, scholars, consultants, books, or periodicals that everyone else doesn't have.

A huge part of their success is the result of solid, down-in-the-trenches, day-after-day, focused execution. As T.J. Rodgers, CEO of Cypress Semiconductor, says, "Most organizations don't fail for lack of strategic vision. They fail for lack of execution."

However, after carefully observing these companies for 20 years, I believe companies that connect the dots are guided by at least three principles, three best principles, if you will.

- They value their people.
- The CEO is the communication champion.
- Communication is managed as a business process.

Let's look at each.

They Value People

Everybody says they value their people. I have wondered if a lot of business leaders in the United States believed that the U.S. Securities and Exchange Commission required them to include "employees are our most valuable resource" in their annual reports. It doesn't, of course, but you couldn't fault someone for suspecting it, given the number of companies that demonstrate every day that they don't give a hoot about their people yet slap references to valuing employees where it will fit.

Towers Perrin conducted a benchmarking study of values-driven companies. All were top performers in their industries. The study demonstrated that the so-called people factor was primary at each company. The most common themes in these values-driven companies were a belief in people as a primary source of competitive advantage, concern for employee well-being, proactive leadership, leadership accountability for effective people management, investment in leadership development, employee involvement, communication effectiveness, program and system alignment, and customer focus. Sound familiar?

Companies that connect the dots are intensely people-focused. They understand that nothing happens inside an organization until someone does something with otherwise inert assets. That computer over on Anne's desk won't do anything until she turns it on. That forklift out in the warehouse will just sit there until Ray hops in it and drives it away. A company won't acquire anyone until Paula makes a decision about who to acquire and then makes a few phone calls. No one will earn anything on their investments until chief financial officer Richard makes an investment.

Companies that connect the dots might as well have a large sign over their front entrances saying: "IT'S THE PEOPLE, STUPID!"

"Doing business is different these days," consultant John Guaspari wrote in *Across the Board*. "The pace, the immediacy, and the interconnectedness of it all make it so. We're not going to win because of our technology, since the ones and zeros in our computer code don't move any faster than the other guy's. We're not going to win on technique—good ideas are more or less infinitely available and eminently transportable. And we know that the old rote, mechanical ways won't give us the edge we're looking for either.

"Instead," Guaspari goes on, "we need to be more institutionally agile and nimble, responsive and adaptive. We must create organizations that are, as the name implies, organic: comfortable with change and embracing an ethos of changing, manifesting the life force that resides only in our people—free moral agents, not cogs in a machine.

"That life force provides the intelligence, zeal, and commitment needed to deal with the happenstance that our models can't predict. Our people have to jump in because there isn't time to wait for 'the answer' to come from on high. And even if time weren't an issue, 'on high' doesn't know 'the answer.' Those who actually do the work— our people—do.

"Here's another thing we all know: Because our people are free moral agents, they will not robotically assent and bring their energy to bear on the situation. Before they do so, the task at hand must be energizing. Otherwise, their tanks will eventually run dry."[3]

Businesses that help people connect the dots and find meaning in their lives understand what Guaspari's talking about.

Great people-focused companies espouse and *live* people-oriented values. For instance, Motorola makes 10 assumptions about people and their relationship with the company. They state:

1. Employee behavior is a consequence of how employees are treated.
2. Employees are intelligent, curious, and responsible.
3. Employees need a rational work world in which they know what's expected of them and why.
4. Employees need to know how their jobs relate to the jobs of others and to company goals.
5. There is only one class of employees, not a creative management group and a group of others who carry out orders.
6. There is no one best way to manage.
7. No one knows how to do his or her job better than the person on the job does.
8. Employees want to have pride in their work.

43

9. Employees want to be involved in decisions that affect their own work.
10. The responsibility of every manager is to draw out the ideas and abilities of workers in a shared effort to address business problems and opportunities.

The HP Way has been an underpinning of Hewlett-Packard's people orientation since its founding. It has three elements: organizational values, corporate objectives, and strategies and practices. The first value is "We have trust and respect for individuals." Having consulted to HP and visited their Palo Alto, California, headquarters on numerous occasions, I know that HP people are absolutely right when they tell you that the HP Way isn't just a poster that's nailed on the wall. People at HP live those values.

Ingram Micro is one of the world's largest technology distributors. It's one of *Fortune*'s "Most Admired Corporations." Jerre Stead is chairman and CEO. He's had a lot to do with Ingram Micro's being on the list. Stead epitomizes the three best principles. He values people, takes the lead in communication, and understands that communication is a process, not a set of activities and events. "Our people are our company's only sustainable competitive advantage," he told me. "When you think of a company, it's only a legal entity. It's a name. That's it. So when people say Ingram Micro, that's just the name of the company. But the people make up the company. The people *are* the company. The only way I know of for a company to be success-ful—to create a great company—is to delight customers, and the only way I know how to do that is with people inside the company."

He continues: "I start out with 100 percent trust. Having this, we are able to create an open environment of people power where you can really open up and create an environment of fulfillment and success for all the associates in the company.

"I want every one of our associates to know they have the tools and training to be successful. I want them to understand the objectives, measures, and reward system. I want them to believe they have the ability to make decisions to meet or exceed their objectives. If we can score an eight or nine on each of those questions on a one to ten scale, we'll blow away the competition."

"You have to believe that you're only as good as the people who work with you," says Larry Weinbach, CEO of Unisys Corporation. "They're going to make you look good or they're going to make you look bad. And part of their making you look good is they've got to feel good, they're got to be motivated, they've got to trust you. I use this word *trust* a lot because I think in business today, employees have to trust the people who are providing leadership."[4]

Companies that value people are different from those that don't. The differences are palpable. You can feel it when you walk in the front door. In people-valuing companies, people look happier. They smile and laugh a lot. There's briskness in their walk. They're nicer, friendlier. They respect each other and you. They're civil. They use good manners. They're interested in what you have to say and expect you to be interested in what they have to say. Because they have a special feeling about their organizations, they believe they're special too. Whether it's in a meeting with Disney, America Online, Hallmark, Toyota, Medtronic, 3M, FedEx, or Ingram Micro, there's something almost fraternal about people's relationships with each other. It's like if you made it onto the team, you must be pretty special. They may not even know you, but because you're one of them, they'll treat you special. Their vocabulary is one of engagement—a lot of "we" and "us." (Have you ever wondered about the degree of connectedness of an employee who refers to the company he's associated with as "they" instead of "we"? Example: You: "Do you have these shoes in a size 9D?" Employee: "I believe *they* do.")

As a consultant, I like the way these companies are considerate of my time and me just as they're considerate of each other and each other's time. They treat me as a valued business partner and as a person rather than as a "vendor" and an outsider.

It's little things like this that in the aggregate make these companies very different.

The CEO Is the Communication Champion

An organization can claim to believe in the value of people, but unless its CEO, the chairman, owner, or ultimate leader is passionate about linking people and what they do to the business goals and strategy, the dots won't connect. The top dog can't will it or fob it off on a function or individual. The ultimate leader has got to passionately drive the effort. Otherwise, the effort isn't sustainable over the long term.

Again, Jerre Stead of Ingram Micro serves as a good model. When I met with Stead in his Santa Ana, California, office, he had just come back from speaking to a group of new Ingram Micro employees at their orientation. Much earlier that day, around 5 a.m., ("The guy never sleeps," one of his colleagues told me.) Stead was in his office responding to e-mail from employees. He maintains his own 24-hour 800-number phone line. He has also given his home phone number to all 13,000 Ingram Micro associates. "My wife answers many of the calls and actually takes care of some situations. I also get 200 to 300 e-mails every day. The total time I take with all the e-mails and phone calls is three hours a day. Eighty percent of that is between five and six o'clock in the morning. I only get one anonymous letter a month," Stead asserts.

"If we are doing something right," Stead says, "I'd love to hear about it. If there's something we should be doing differently, I want to know that too."

"The leader has to develop the kind of environment where the employees want to work and be happy in their work, and I don't know how you can do it if you aren't a good communicator and people don't have faith in what you're saying," Larry Weinbach of Unisys says.

"I use communication as my way of getting people to understand what I call 'the X factor,' the success factor that is going to be built around how well all these 33,000 people are motivated to do what I believe they have the ability to do," Weinbach adds.[5]

When Richard Brown took over as CEO of Electronic Data Systems, he said he needed to accelerate communication. "I'm not Edgar Allan Poe and I'm not trying to be Albert Einstein," Brown said. "I want [EDS people] to hear what's on Dick Brown's mind. I learn a lot from the tons of responses I get."[6]

Jack Welch, Chairman of GE, *Fortune's* most admired company, is another communication role model. "Leadership means more vision, more communication," Welch says. "We like people who are passionate about what they're doing… who have a vision about where they want to go… and can communicate that vision to the people they want to get there with."

Welch is a master at managing communication to connect people to the business: "I think, very simply, that communication means everybody having the same set of facts. When people of the same basic intelligence get the same information, they come to similar conclusions within a small band."

And he wants everyone on board and connected. "I just believe that we [are] going to have to be far more competitive, and the only way to be more competitive [is] to engage every mind in the organization. You can't have anybody on the sidelines," Welch insists.

And regarding Web technology, Welch says, "We will never again have discussions where knowledge is hidden in someone's pocket. You have to lead with ideas, not by controlling information."

Jim Orr, president of UNUM prior to its recent merger with Provident, offers frank guidance to would-be CEOs: "If you aren't willing to take the lead by getting out with the people—not to put spin on the messages but to openly and honestly communicate—you shouldn't be a CEO."

Irv Hockaday at Hallmark Cards pounds away at the value of people and the importance of communication. "A CEO's primary responsibilities are to provide vision, to motivate employees, and to develop leaders," Hockaday says. "To do that requires communication—open, frequent, and flowing both from the top down and the bottom up. It's the responsibility of the CEO not just to listen and communicate with employees but to foster an environment in which everyone else does the same.[7]

Larry Bossidy, Chairman of AlliedSignal, a *Fortune* most admired company, tells his managers, "We can't be a premier company without premier communication—the kind of communication that leads to... a feeling of ownership and business results. We must talk with—and listen to—each other all the time, at every opportunity, and about everything that affects the business and the experience of working here if we are to become a premier company. I want us to act like everyone in this company is the world's best at what they do. And as such, everyone has a right to be heard as well as an obligation to contribute. Employees want to do their best, but they can't if they don't understand our goals and what they must do to accomplish them. In fact, every employee should understand the business so well that they need little direction to excel; they should act and feel like owners."

Open communication—linking people and what they do to the business doesn't happen by accident. It starts with leadership. It's driven home with leadership.

Communication Is Managed as a Business Process

When many business people think about communication, they think of it first as a collection of activities, events, and formal media that emanate from the hierarchical top and spew downward into the organization. They think of information dissemination *to* people rather than communication *among* people, "telling them what they need to know" versus creating clarity and building shared meaning.

To bring about clarity and build shared meaning communication must be managed as a business process, just as planning, engineering, manufacturing and distribution must be managed as business processes. The communication process, however, is different from other processes. It spans all the other processes. It weaves its way throughout all of them, just as radio signals can permeate every corner of your house. In other words, planning, engineering, manufacturing, and distribution can't work without communication. If you're a doubter, try it. For one day, do not permit a single word, signal, cue, sign, symbol, facial expression, or twitch of the body to happen within one of those processes. Then tell me how well that process is working. It won't. It can't. Communication is a process to be managed lest other processes become flawed.

Jack Welch will tell you what communication isn't and what it is. "It's not a speech… or a videotape. It's not a plant newspaper. Real communication is an attitude, an environment. It's the most interactive of all processes. It requires countless hours of eyeball-to-eyeball back and forth. It is a constant, interactive process aimed at creating consensus."

Leaders will often nod their heads in agreement that communication is a process that they need to manage. But when communication breaks down or otherwise becomes flawed, they often reach for the nearest available and easiest "solution." They call their communication people and order up a video or a story in the employee publication. Never mind the fact that the absence of a video or story in the employee publication has never to my knowledge influenced a key performance measure one scintilla. But producing a video or writing a story for a publication is easy and we all want easy.

Once, when conducting a communication symposium for a group of managers during a merger, one of the managers cornered me during a break and said he was disappointed that I was not addressing communication as much as he had anticipated. I asked him what he thought I had been talking about for the past two hours. "You've been talking more about business than communication," he told me. He was right. But what he didn't understand was that you can't separate the communication process from the rest of the business.

You can't not communicate. It's going to happen whether you want it to or think it should. It's like the wind when you're sailing. You have the choice of ignoring it or managing it. Sailboats tend to sail better when you don't ignore the wind. Businesses tend to run better when you don't ignore communication.

CHAPTER 4

Leadership: Making the Weather

Never doubt the capacity of the people you lead to accomplish whatever you dream for them.

— Ben Zander, conductor, Boston Philharmonic Orchestra

C ompanies that connect the dots know that the secret lies in managing the communication bombardment. That means they first have to understand the sources of the bombardment where all those cues, signals, signs, messages, and data come from. That way, they will know *what* to manage. They know there are three primary sources:

- Leadership
- Systems infrastructure
- Formal communication media

In this and the next two chapters, we'll look at each of the three communication sources shown in Figure 4-1 and discuss the impact

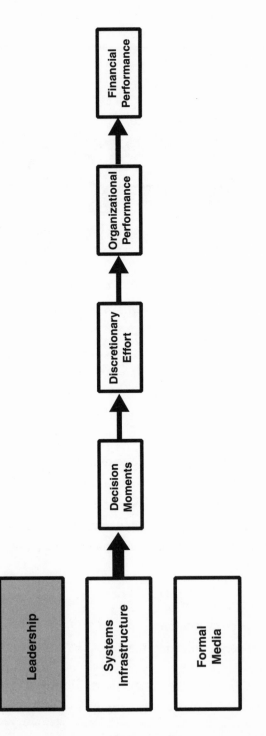

Figure 4-1. The sources of communication.

each has on decision moments and the actions people take when they exercise discretionary effort.

"What most influences what you decide to do every day?" I once asked a group of scientists in Minneapolis. Similarly, I asked a group of poultry processing people in Maryland, "How do you decide what to do?" These two groups seemed different in every way except how they answered this question. "The boss." "Our manager." "My supervisor." "Top management." "Leaders." Those were the responses from both groups.

Leadership. People with *position power*. Leaders can be CEOs, managers, or supervisors. Or they can be simply *top management*, a term that's perceived differently by different people. To some, top management means about three levels up from where they are in the hierarchy. To others, it means the head of a plant, a division, or a branch office. And to some, it's the ultimate leader, the CEO or owner.

Leaders can be people with *personal power*. They're people others gravitate to regardless of their position or job title. They're the people who others go to and ask, "What do you think?" or "What's really going on?" When these leaders speak, others nod in agreement. These are the natural leaders. Every organization has natural leaders. Sometimes, natural leaders can persuade people to follow the company line. Sometimes, they can persuade people to join a union.

Leaders set the tone. My friend Roger D'Aprix, one of the world's leading communication consultants, often tells of an employee he encountered in a focus group who explained boss power in no uncertain terms. Quite simply, the employee told D'Aprix, "The boss makes the weather."

Go to any grocery store that's part of a large national chain, and you'll see how the store manager's personality can be felt everywhere. The store's performance will track closely with the quality of store management. Stay in a Hilton, Holiday Inn, Marriott, or Ritz Carlton. The general manager's presence is everywhere. It takes on his or her personality. The great grocery and lodging chains know this and invest huge amounts of time, energy, and money developing their store managers and general managers.

People watch what leaders say and what they don't say, what they do and how they act. We notice where they sit, where they park, what's first and last on their agendas, questions they ask, and questions they don't ask. We watch their body language. We note their tone of voice and facial expressions. We pay close attention to what they wear, who they promote, who they ignore. Everything a leader says and does is scrutinized for meaning, because everything a leader says or does assumes importance as a form of communication, often far beyond even what the leader imagines. And we react.

John Onoda, who heads communication at VISA USA, tells how he tries to help his leaders understand that it's what they do rather than what they say that people pay attention to.

"I tell top management to think of themselves as actors in a silent movie," Onoda says. "No one can hear a word you're saying. You have to communicate completely through your actions. You have no words, only behavior with which to communicate."[8]

People who've recently assumed significant leadership positions often express surprise that they've suddenly entered a fishbowl, in which even personal habits become messages about what's important. John S., the newly appointed head of a division of a large agrochemical company, told me he couldn't believe how people were reacting to him. "I can't believe how everybody hangs on to everything I say. They notice everything. They read meaning into things I didn't intend. I'm starting to get so careful about what I do. I'm getting tentative, sort of afraid I'll send the wrong meaning. It's very uncomfortable, but I guess it comes with the territory. I've got to be careful about what I do."

Richard Champion, an officer at Florida Progress, an electric utility, said when he was promoted from director to vice president, "My whole world changed. It was one of the strangest things. The job title changed, but the job and amount of authority I had didn't. I had just as much or just as little authority before the job title changed. But people treated me very differently."

People watch everything for meaning, and in the process they discover some of the tiniest things that scream out messages about a leader's preferences, priorities, and moods.

Larry Weinbach tells a story about the buzz he inadvertently created the first day he was CEO at Unisys Corporation: "As I was walking down the hall, I opened a door and a young lady was coming out carrying a computer. She had a piece of paper to give to the guard. As I opened the door, this piece of paper fell because of the breeze. I picked it up, held the door for her, and gave it to the guard. I went off on my business and she went out to her car.

"When I got back to my office, my secretary said, 'What did you do?' I said, 'I don't know what you mean.' And she replied, 'We have all these e-mails from employees thanking you for helping this young lady.'

"At the time, it didn't mean much to me, but when I got home that night, I said to my wife, 'You know, this company is weird. Why would anybody thank you for doing something that you would naturally do?'"

Sometimes, it's the little things that speak loudest. For example:

Jack is chairman of an insurance company. Everyone in the company knows that when Jack gets bored during a presentation or discussion, he reaches for his nail clippers and begins cleaning or trimming his nails, whether they need it or not. So, when Jack reaches for his nail clippers, people quickly end their presentations or change the subject. They know he's bored. He's turned the presenter off.

Dick is the chairman of a transportation company. He has a

habit of rolling his eyes a certain way when he disagrees with someone. People who meet with Dick keep an eye on Dick's eyes. His eyes communicate loudly.

Buster runs a branch operation of a financial services company. He always comes to the office on Sunday. Before he headed the branch, no one came to the office on Sunday. Now the office is packed with people on Sundays. Buster says he never told anyone that he expected people to come to the office on Sundays. But they do, in hordes. When Buster comes to the office on Sunday, he communicates his work ethic. His managers think if they come to the office on Sundays, it will communicate that they share Buster's work ethic. They think this mutual sharing of work ethic will get them ahead at work. "Funny thing is," Buster says, "I started coming to the office on Sundays because it was the only quiet time I could find. I started coming here to get some work done. It was the only time I wouldn't be interrupted. I guess they thought I thought because I'm here, they should be here. But that wasn't my intent. I was looking for some peace and quiet."

The chairman of a food products company regularly allows himself to be interrupted by telephone calls in meetings. He often gets up and leaves in the middle of someone's discussion or presentation. All his managers know it's rude behavior. One manager described the chairman as "boorish." "But we're all starting to do it," he added, "because he communicates that it's okay."

Many business leaders ask if there are certain behaviors that employees watch most to determine whether leaders are authentic or whether they're just engaged in a passing fad. What, they ask, do the best leaders do that has the greatest impact?

I've interviewed thousands of employees in every conceivable industry. Here's what they say they watch. Here's how they decide whether you're real, or that you're serious. They tell me the following actions communicate the loudest.

- What you take the lead on (some call it role modeling)
- What you spend time on
- How well you listen
- Who you reward and recognize
- How you use symbolism

Taking the Lead

"When will you know the company's serious about cutting costs?" I asked a group of employees gathered around the conference table of a midwestern retailer.

"When management cuts their costs," an employee shot back.

"When will you know the leadership's serious about changing the culture?" I asked a group of bank employees gathered in a hotel room in Toronto.

"When the president and his top management walk the talk," they fired back.

I've asked the "when will you know..." question more than a thousand times, and more than a thousand times, people have answered the same: "When leadership goes first."

In their superior book on leadership, entitled *Credibility,* Jim Kouzes and Barry Posner write about going first:

> Leaders take the first step because doing so demonstrates their faith in the idea, program, or service. Going first provides tangible evidence of the leader's commitment. It demonstrates the leader's willingness to experiment and learn from the inevitable mistakes of trying out new concepts. What the leader does is the single most important factor in demonstrating to others what is acceptable—and unacceptable—behavior in our organizations.

By taking the lead, leaders communicate that others have permission to do the same things. But when leaders talk about cost control on Monday and fly to Scotland to grouse hunt at company expense on Tuesday (as one of my clients did), is it any wonder that their credibility plummets?

Using Your Time

How you use time signals your priorities. What you do and how you do it tells everyone around you what's important and what's not important to you.

Think about what you did at 2 p.m. yesterday. Did it help you communicate what you wanted to communicate? Look at your calendar for the last 30 days. Did it communicate the values and priorities that you want to communicate to your people?

Ben G., the president of a health care insurance company, spent a lot of time telling his people how important the customers were to the future of the company. Although he preached customer service and responsiveness, his employees didn't think he was serious. When asked to review what he had done during the past 30 days, he was shocked.

"I'm embarrassed at what my calendar says about me," he confessed. "It says I think administrative minutiae is really important. I can't believe what I let myself get into."

Ben, therefore, began managing his calendar more strategically, using it to communicate what was really important to him. Focus groups two months afterward revealed a shift in the perceptions of his top management team. "Ben's much more focused now," one said. "He's getting his point across much better."

A *BusinessWeek* article on GE's Jack Welch reported that Welch spends 15 to 20 percent of his time interacting with customers, and more than 50 percent of his time on people issues.

Effectively, the leader's behavior is the model we use to determine or calibrate our own behaviors and choices. It's not just the big decisions (for example, should we open or close a plant?) that set the example. Hundreds of little opportunities each day can provide more telling examples of what our leaders do or don't stand for.

Communicating by Listening

The power of asking…

If you preach the importance of customer satisfaction but always ask people about their production numbers, should you be surprised if they think you put production first and customer satisfaction second?

Leadership scholar and author Warren Bennis says his research proves that successful leaders tend to be askers of great questions. "They want to know what and why. And they are superb listeners, particularly to those who advocate new or different images of emerging reality. That's how they stay on the leading edge of change."

As UNUM's former CEO Jim Orr says, "[T]he ability to listen as a member of a team [and] the concepts of teamwork and collaboration are becoming more important. We have to be able to listen—and learn—from business associates. Yet listening is a lot more difficult than speaking."

When Hallmark CEO Irv Hockaday participates in a meeting of Hallmarkers, as the company's employees are called, he asks a lot of questions. He usually begins meetings with a brief discussion of Hallmark's vision and business strategy. He then peppers the group with questions, questions that communicate his priorities. For example, at one such meeting he asked:

- What are our customers saying about us?
- What do we need to do for our customers that we're not doing?

- What do I need to do or stop doing to help you realize your full potential—to be the best you can be? What's in your way?
- How can we be more creative?
- How can we get our costs down and make our processes faster?

Hallmarkers walk away from Hockaday meetings knowing precisely what's important to him: employees, customers, creativity, costs, and speed. And they know he knows that his job is to help clear the way so they can be their best.

Contrast Hockaday's approach to the typical CEO performance. The typical CEO gives his speech and then asks for and answers employee questions, because he perceives himself, not the employees, as the source of all the answers. These are the same CEOs who wonder why the company is possessed with a we/they attitude.

People in organizations don't miss any of this. Take the case of two women who cofacilitated a key strategy meeting among their peers. When Sue facilitated the session, she talked a lot, forcefully stating her opinion about everything. She was articulate and to herself probably sounded very wise. Beth, on the other hand, was a master facilitator. She had opinions, but she spent most of her facilitation time encouraging others. She asked insightful questions. She probed. When Sue facilitated, members of the group sat and listened—or feigned listening. When Beth facilitated the group, the group came alive, offering ideas on every subject that was addressed. While Sue was impressive when she spoke, in the end, the parts of the meeting she facilitated weren't productive. Not much new was put on the table. When Beth facilitated, the meeting was at its most productive.

At the end of the session, one meeting participant whispered to me: "Sue tries to get the best out of herself; Beth tries to bring out the best in others." The fact is, Sue didn't and Beth did.

Listening and asking the right questions communicates forcefully.

"Credibility is earned through human contact—in the hallways, on the factory floors, in the retail shops, in the classrooms, and on the streets," Kouzes and Posner write in *Credibility*. "Credible leaders take the time to listen and learn."

Andy Grove, Intel's chairman, spends a lot of time on the factory floor just talking and asking. "Think of what happens when someone comes to see a manager in his office," Grove explains. "A certain stop-and-start dynamic occurs when the visitor sits down. While a two-minute kernel of information is exchanged, the meeting often takes a half-hour. But if a manager walks through an area and sees a person with whom he has a two-minute concern, he can simply stop, cover his subject, and be on his way."[9]

Ben Zander, conductor of the Boston Philharmonic Orchestra, says he "listens" with his eyes. "One way to check whether I'm doing an adequate job is to look in my musicians' eyes," Zander says. "The eyes never lie. If the eyes are shining, then I know that my leadership is working. Human beings in the presence of possibility react physically as well as emotionally. If the eyes aren't shining, I ask myself, 'What am I doing that's keeping my musicians' eyes from shining?' That question also works for the transformation of the dominating father—'What kind of parent am I being that my children's eyes aren't shining?'—or the dominating teacher or the dominating manager."[10]

Signaling What's Important Through Rewards and Recognition

When someone new is named to head a business, everybody watches what the new leader does. One of the loudest—but often unspoken—questions is Who's going to get the top jobs? First of all, "who gets the jobs" communicates who won or lost in the leadership change. But we also look at each of the new appointees to try to figure out what's *really* important and unimportant to the new leader.

John Reed, CEO of Citicorp, addressed this issue shortly after his company and Travelers merged to form Citigroup. "Let's be straight," Reed told reporters, "two people sharing a job is inherently difficult. Everybody in our organization will be looking at the two of us (Reed and Travelers' CEO Sanford Weill), measuring the size of my office, measuring the size of his, trying to figure who is doing what to whom."

A few years ago, I was helping an electric power company in the southwest prepare for new competitive issues brought on by deregulation. The president and the various employee communication vehicles hammered away at the need to be innovative, to break out of the old regulated mindset. The president told employees to try new things, think out of the box, and take risks. But employees weren't buying it.

"Why?" I asked. One brave soul spoke for a group of employees. "We've heard him talk," he said, referring to the president. "We've read all the articles. We've seen the videos. But it's all bogus."

"Why is it all bogus?" I asked.

"The phoniness started when Cooper (the CEO) appointed the former finance guy to executive vice president, the number-two position and next in line to be president," the employee explained. "This guy's the classic old-line white male in his fifties who's known as a survivor. He's never had an original idea in his life. He's steeped in regulation. He's cautious, conservative, and doesn't give a damn about people. We're not going to change a bit with him there. Cooper's dreaming."

Business leaders must consider the messages they send when they appoint people to positions. Does the appointment communicate what should be communicated?

When a leader gives Jennifer a 20-year service pin, he's communicating that loyalty or length of service is important. When he gives Lindsay $5000 for an innovative idea that almost worked but eventually flopped and says, "Keep trying," he's communicating to all the

Lindsays in the company that it's okay to keep stretching and trying, even if it means that you don't succeed every time.

Promoting Andrew over Chuck and Terry communicates that Andrew represents someone closer to the leader's "ideal" than Chuck or Terry. People will get the message, and they'll surmise that being more like Andrew is more desirable than being more like Chuck or Terry.

A leader can talk diversity all day, even hire a black female head of diversity. But promote a black female to head worldwide manufacturing and you're really walking your diversity talk.

Using the Power of Symbolism

No one seems to miss anything a leader says or does. The danger associated with this is that people read all kinds of unintended meanings into things leaders do. I'm often reminded of the phrase, "Your actions speak so loudly, I can hardly hear what you're saying."

The great leaders carefully, yet sincerely, manage what they do to communicate what they want. They manage symbolism well.

Glen Hiner is chairman of Owens Corning. One of the telling acts of his leadership was to move the company's headquarters down the street and over next to the Maumee River. That's perhaps not a big deal by itself until you compare the old and the new.

For years, Owens Corning's headquarters were in a 28-story building in downtown Toledo. Top management sat on the 28th floor. If an employee or customer accidentally pushed the wrong button and found himself nudged upward to the 28th floor, they usually wouldn't get far. The high ceilings, deep carpet, pricey artwork, and lack of observable workers would immediately intimidate them back onto the elevator.

Hiner told me he got his idea about moving corporate headquarters when he was riding up the elevator with some Owens Corning employees. As the employees started to get off on their floors, Hiner invited them to come up and see him. Here's how he described their response: "The two of them looked at me and said, 'Why in the world would anyone on their own want to go up to the 28th floor? You've got to be crazy.' Leaving the leadership up there on the 28th floor sent a clear signal: We didn't want to be where the action was; we didn't want to be bothered; we wanted to be out of touch. Of course, that wasn't true. But it sent that message."

So Hiner built a new building. It's as if the company took the 28-story building, wheeled it down the street to the river, and then carefully laid it over on its side.

But the Owens Corning building is a lot more than a new building in downtown Toledo. While the 28-story building communicated the importance of hierarchy and gave an impression of management aloofness, the company's new three-story building and open environment clearly communicate the importance of teamwork, collaboration, learning, sharing, and technology.

Hiner eschewed a corner office and a personal parking space, telling space designers that walking through the parking lot and having his office in the middle of the action gave him a better opportunity to communicate with company employees. He's not far from the employee cafeteria, and he eats there when he's in town. The day I met with him, he asked a small group if they minded if he joined them for lunch. They didn't and he did.

Employees tell me that what leaders say and do manages decision moments and that employees use those moments more than any other communication sources. The best leaders use this to their advantage. They manage what they say and do to communicate their values, the culture they're trying to build, and the actions they want people to take.

CHAPTER 5

Systems Speak

*The greatest problem with communication is
the illusion that it has been accomplished.*

— George Bernard Shaw

I f what leaders do communicates powerfully, their power is rivaled only by that of the systems infrastructure.

The systems infrastructure is like the plumbing, electrical, heating, air conditioning, and framing systems in our homes. In our businesses, it includes all of the processes, systems, structure, policies, procedures, and programs that govern operations. It includes workplace architecture, the physical environment, organizational structure, pay systems, measurement systems, goal setting, succession management, financial and planning processes, employee benefits, resource allocation systems, information systems, and many more (see Figure 5-1).

When a business is small, it doesn't need a lot of infrastructure. At the end of each day, owners just pay each other with what's left over. There aren't any fancy pay plans. There's little, if any, organizational structure. The term *performance management* often isn't even used in small companies. But as businesses grow, they need some

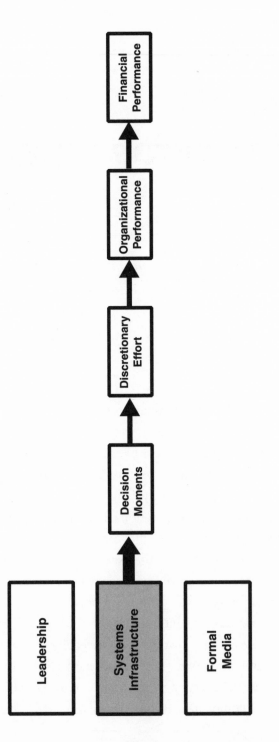

Figure 5-1. The second communication source and how it affects the path to performance.

infrastructure just to hold the organization together. Too little infrastructure can retard growth. Too much can promote cumbersome bureaucracy, which also retards growth. The key is to impose the right amount of infrastructure in order to support and foster continued growth and performance. As the head of human resources for a technology company put it, "We want to fuel growth by preserving what got us here in the first place, but we know we need to install some structure to avoid chaos in the extreme. That's a difficult balance to create."

The infrastructure can take on a life of its own. Some of it is the legacy of earlier leaders of the organization, who move on but leave their structural offerings behind. Some of it is the result of leaders who telegraph their values and behaviors to the rest of the organization over time, making a kind of cultural deposit in the organization's bank account. Some of it is the result of programmatic fiddling over time. The good folks in human resources revise a pay plan. Six months later, the finance people create a new cost accounting method. A year goes by and marketing installs a new customer satisfaction data collection process, while operations is refining its work processes. HR worries about HR systems. Finance worries about the processes it owns. Marketing and operations tend to their issues. But all too often, there isn't anyone worrying about how all of these systems work from the overall company perspective.

Over time, then, the various systems that make up the infrastructure can begin to work at odds with one another. And all of it communicates loudly, often cacophonously, as leftover policies and programs, seemingly from as far back as the Flood, come into conflict.

Systems speak, some blatantly such as a policy that explains the proper process to use to order office supplies. But that same policy might also communicate subtler messages. For instance, let's assume that Mary Frances, who is otherwise trusted to manage 10 people and a $3 million portfolio of business, is instructed by that policy to secure five signatures prior to submitting a $1000 order for office supplies. What does this policy communicate to Mary Frances about how much the organization trusts her? Might it conflict with other messages that we send about how much we trust and value people? If you think like most employees, the answer is, "Of course!"

The infrastructure's many systems need to be aligned in order to communicate consistently. That is, they all need to "say" the same thing. What they say needs to guide people when they encounter decision moments. What they say needs to drive behavior toward winning. Every system communicates, however, five big systems have emerged that seem to communicate loudest to people, thereby driving their decision moments and the actions they take. They are:

- Structure
- Measurement and rewards
- Policies and procedures
- Resource allocation
- Working environment

Let's look at how each has the opportunity to send consistent or mixed messages that influence performance.

Structure

Structure represents the way we organize our business to do work. It's the "boxology" of business that's often represented by the organization chart. It includes reporting relationships, accountabilities, hierarchic levels, and titles. It's the "who reports to whom" piece of any business.

Organizational structure represents our formal documented processes for communicating with each other. It organizes how we do our work and establishes how we make decisions. Some structures run deep, with many levels. Some are flat. There are virtual structures, spider web structures, matrix structures, process-focused structures, and hundreds of permutations of each. Sometimes, multiple structures reside in the same organization.

Structures affect communication directly and indirectly.

Structure can directly influence whether and how information flows inside the organization. It can influence direction, speed, and accuracy.

In the traditional level-conscious organization, where position in the hierarchy represents one's presumed importance, communication was typically managed down through the hierarchy, one level at a time. Vice presidents received information before directors, directors before managers, managers before supervisors, and supervisors before the people who did real work. Technology has speeded up the world. It has replaced many of the levels that were established, in part, to move information.

Honoring the hierarchy by cascading information is an obsolete way to manage communication. It's slow, time-consuming, and expensive. Every level represents an opportunity to distort or drop information. It doesn't contribute to improved quality, speedy service, or lower costs. It doesn't get information to people who need it at twitch speed.

In today's fast-paced, connected, engaged organizations, people should communicate with whomever they need to communicate whenever they need to do so. Level shouldn't matter. Only results should matter. Name any high-performance team in any field of endeavor where the players are required to communicate with a dozen intermediaries to get results.

"The vertical processing of information is the slowest cycle in any organization," says Jim Manzi, former Lotus Notes CEO and now head of Nets Inc. Robert Buckman, CEO of Buckman Laboratories, agrees: "You can't go up to a guru and then back down the way we used to. It's too slow; you lose relevant detail."[11]

Structure also communicates indirectly. A deep structure by itself can communicate that speed isn't important and that position in the hierarchy is more important than position in the marketplace. Its very presence communicates what's valued.

A manufacturing company required its sales force to secure approvals for price reductions from the marketing department in the company's corporate headquarters. The salesperson had to make the request to her manager, who took it to a district manager, who took it to a regional manager, who called corporate marketing, often only to find that the corporate marketing person who could okay the price reduction was in an all-day meeting and couldn't be disturbed. By the time the marketing person who could make the decision sent her approval back through the hierarchy, the salesperson many times had lost the sale to a competitor whose employee in the field was informed, engaged, and able to make the right pricing decision on the spot.

Members of the sales force expressed frustration over this process. But what the sales force was truly angry about was the fact that they believed the company had lost its competitive drive and its focus on the customer. "It's like we don't care about getting the business any more," one salesperson told me.

The company's leadership may have been claiming that it cared about the customer. All of their speeches may have made references to being more customer-focused. The posters, banners, and memos may have said the customer was important. But the structure communicated that winning the business through a quick, accurate response wasn't a high priority. The structure won.

Structure also wins when businesses are divided into vertical silos and people in one department have difficulty communicating with those in another. In some businesses, people at one level aren't permitted (or at least it's discouraged) to call or talk to people at higher levels. These barriers are artificial. They impede communication and reduce performance.

Here's another anecdote. It really happened. Bob W., the head of communication for a media organization, was an old timer, very traditional, a staunch adherent to the rules. A member of his staff, Mary K., was extremely bright and insightful, possessed solid business acumen, and was valued for her good judgment. Bob invited me to a meeting to discuss a major communication issue with this organization's CEO. I asked Bob who would be at the meeting. He told me. Mary was missing from the invitation list, so I suggested that she be invited.

"Well, I think you're right. She would be good to have, but she'd be the only manager level in the room," Bob explained. "This is pretty much a meeting of VPs."

I had an easy and only partially tongue-in-cheek solution. "So why don't you quickly make her a VP before the meeting. Then demote her after the meeting. It's not her title we want. We want her brains."

Bob thought my idea was as crazy as it sounded and said curtly, "That just wouldn't work in this company." My obviously absurd suggestion was lost on him.

Structure won out again. In this case, it deprived the meeting of Mary's competence. Given my knowledge of the other meeting participants, Mary's absence represented a huge gulf.

Measurement and Rewards

What counts is what you count. What gets rewarded gets done. Both notions have been part of the corporate discussion for years. Yet, many business leaders suffer the drag caused by measurement and reward systems that are grossly out of alignment with what's needed to win. They simply communicate the wrong messages—messages that are inconsistent with driving people and what they do in the right direction.

When people don't seem to be doing what's needed to win, you might start your culprit search by first looking at how effectively measurement is being used in the goal-setting process.

During an engagement with a mid-Atlantic utility, the head of human resources told me of the CEO's frustration with his own leadership team. "I've watched them when they work together," the head of HR told me. "They're polite. They nod their heads. They agree. Then they leave the meeting and do what they want to do. Why is this?" she asked.

I asked whether these leaders shared common performance goals. Are they, I asked, measured on their contribution to each other's success and does the CEO hold them accountable for hitting their targets? I asked. Her reply: "No and no."

She had her answer—no common performance goals or measures, no accountability. The company's measurement and rewards process for these leaders was designed to produce precisely the kind of behavior it was getting from its leadership team. It communicated that working together as a team wasn't important. The measurement and rewards system had spoken and the leaders had listened.

While I was speaking on the subject of leadership communication at a conference in San Francisco, a questioner in the back of the room raised her hand and asked: "I've been trying to get our line managers to understand the importance of communication. It's not working. What do you recommend?"

I asked two basic questions: What do these folks get measured on? And, what do they get rewarded and recognized for?

"Making their numbers," she responded.

Are they making their numbers? I asked. "No, we're having serious financial problems," she replied.

I asked her if the managers were measured on *how* they're supposed to make their numbers. For instance, I asked: "Are they measured on the environments they create, on employee evaluations of their leadership qualities, or on their ability to build and foster open communication?"

"No, not at all," she replied.

"Well," I suggested, "I'd start there." When the managers understand that open communication is a tool to help them make their numbers and that they're being held accountable for the means and the ends, they'll be more apt to focus on both making the numbers and the communication environment that's needed to achieve high performance.

While measurement is a crucial element of the goal-setting and accountability process, by itself it can have a significant impact on what people do.

FedEx, for example, uses large red scoreboards in its hub operations to make it clear to everyone that on-time delivery is critical.

Ingram Micro, the world's leading wholesale distributor of technology products and services, receives 50,000 calls a day. Their 500 telemarketers can glance at electronic bulletin boards and learn the number of customer calls waiting in a queue, the average time spent answering a customer call, and the number of abandoned calls. The numbers focus on taking care of customers.

The wrong measurement can produce unwanted results, although the goals and intentions may be right. For instance, some leaders say they want to build a learning environment but only measure the numbers of hours or dollars they allocate to training and development. Allocating time and money to training and development ensures that you'll devote resources to training, but it doesn't guarantee anyone will learn anything.

Some companies still measure success in part by "employee satisfaction" scores, but neglect to define satisfaction properly. For instance, if your employees are attracted to your company because of its traditional, paternalistic values and you're trying to shift from a culture of paternalism to one of engagement, you shouldn't be trying to increase employee satisfaction. Increasing satisfaction could only perpetuate the old culture. Instead, you should measure something different from employee satisfaction, such as commitment or engagement. Engagement and commitment assessments measure different things than employee satisfaction assessments measure.

Some companies wanting to create a team environment measure success by the number of teams they have. A large chemical company did just that. They generated a lot of meetings and a lot of activity but not much real teamwork. They certainly didn't get the results that real teamwork might have helped provide. Measuring the number of teams in operation almost brought a large division of the company to a grinding halt. Nothing was getting done. The conference rooms, however, were booked to capacity.

Some companies say they want to improve face-to-face communication, so they measure managers and supervisors on the number of meetings they conduct or speeches they give. They get what they measure—a lot of activity—but they might not improve communication at all. In fact, poorly prepared or poorly skilled line managers can do more damage than good by having more meetings rather than fewer.

Reward systems represent a sister system to measurement. Each is powerful. Often, they work together to create success or chaos.

A couple of years ago a global construction materials company was trying to engage its field employees. The people in the field worked in rock quarries and gravel and cement-making operations. The head of quality told me that the field people "just show up, do as little as possible, and then go home." He added, "They act as though they just get paid for showing up."

"How *are* these folks paid?" I asked.

"By the hour. They get an hourly wage," the head of quality answered.

"Any incentive pay, profit sharing, or the like?" I asked.

"No."

"Then," I told my client, "it seems to me that they're doing exactly what their pay plan is communicating that they should do. They're showing up and getting rewarded for doing so."

Hourly wages pay people for their time: work one hour, get $10;

74

work two hours, get $20. The hourly wage communicates only that an employee needs to show up and he'll get paid for the time he puts in. It doesn't communicate the importance of producing great quality, holding down costs, or looking for new ways to work smarter. Hourly wages communicate one thing: be there. What you're supposed to do while you're there isn't often discussed in an hourly wage plan.

Federal law requires that certain people be paid hourly and be eligible for overtime pay. Many union contracts focus on hourly wages, although more are starting to include incentives for improving performance. If you must pay people by the hour, there are a lot of ways to supplement hourly wage plans with incentives and recognition designed to communicate that performance is important. If you don't have to pay people hourly, look for creative ways to use the reward system to communicate that performance is important. Connect people to the business strategy by letting them know how they can contribute to a healthier enterprise and by letting them know how they'll benefit when they do. Base salaries communicate that you trust people and how *they* decide to use their time. Hourly wages don't.

"We're told that quality, productivity, safety, and cost-control are tickets to our success," an employee in an auto manufacturing company told me. "But our 10 percent performance bonus is 10 percent every year, no matter what. There's no change, regardless of how well we do on quality, productivity, safety, or cost-control." The performance bonus process in this company was communicating that people were *entitled* to an additional 10 percent hit above their base pay every year. But it was no more than that, an entitlement. The company was missing an opportunity to reinforce its performance messages through the system.

An important part of the concept of total rewards is recognition. Although most businesses have some form of formalized pay or reward scheme, many have not thought through the immense value of recognition programs that are carefully aligned with the company's strategic objectives. As a result, employees' recognition tanks, so to speak, are often empty. There's a lot to be gained from well thought out recognition initiatives.

The fast-growing, immensely successful Medtronic is one of the best at recognition. This member of *Fortune's* "Most Admired" list heaps huge amounts of recognition on the people that make the company successful. Minneapolis-based Medtronic makes lifesaving equipment, such as pacemakers.

While working with the folks at Medtronic, I've had a lot of opportunities to trek to the company's second-floor cafeteria. On the way is a huge area that might as well have been called the Hall of Heroes. One wall is adorned with patent award plaques, another with the Star of Excellence for customer-focused quality. Another wall celebrates leadership with the Wallin Leadership Award. The Global Cup and President's Cup recognize sales people, and the prestigious Bakken Society (Earle Bakken founded Medtronic) acknowledges scientific contributions. All the things that have made Medtronic one of the world's highest performing companies are ensconced there together.

Contrast that with companies that still allocate their wall space to 30-year service anniversaries. "There's old Mildred right up there with all the others who stuck it out for 30 years," my host and guide at a utility told me. "She never much liked her work, always went home right on time, griped and groaned and hated her work. But she kept showing up for work the next day. So we put her picture up there on the wall with all the rest."

Policies and Procedures

We need policies, procedures, and documented work processes to assure consistent quality and service and to work safely, as the head of any chemical plant or nuclear facility will tell you—with passion. Reliable methods ensure that people use the same processes to help guarantee reliability. It's not profitable for people in a company to reinvent the wheel every time they do what someone in another part of the company did yesterday. We need policies and procedures to communicate expectations and standards.

In a speed-driven world, though, where customer demands and standards seem to shift daily, people also need the latitude to make decisions quickly. We can't expect them to "do it the way they've always done it" if it's no longer the best way to do it, or if the way they've always done it has become irrelevant to business needs.

By their very presence, cumbersome policies and procedures manuals can communicate that you're seeking rigidity and conformity, when instead, you may want to be communicating the importance of managing change well, fostering agility, and becoming a more adaptive organization.

An insurance company I recently worked with established as one of its eight performance goals the requirement to comply with business policies and all standards of business conduct. Presumably, the more people complied, the better they'd do in the company. The employees told me they were slaves to the company's operating guidelines and that the company's rigidity prevented them from serving customers. Another goal was to become a learning organization, an irony prompting one of its agents to ask, "How can we learn to be agile and flexible and customer-focused if we also have to comply with all the policies?"

Sometimes policies communicate the right messages; sometimes they don't.

A burner in the furnace at a large entertainment company quit working one cold winter morning. Joe, the company's maintenance foreman, had two choices. Option one was to go down the street to a supply store, purchase a replacement burner for $300, and replace the burner in the furnace—total elapsed time: about three hours; total cost: $300 and perhaps some cab fare to and from the supply store.

Option two was the one the company's policy manual dictated. It said the maintenance foreman needed to request (in writing, of course) a purchase order for the new burner from the finance department. The purchase order needed five signatures, including the signature of the chief operating officer. After all the signatures were secured, the maintenance foreman could then go down to the supply store, purchase the new burner, return to the company's furnace room, and install the burner—total elapsed time: 10 days; total cost: $1200, including cab fare, the price of the burner, and administrative cost associated with securing forms and management signatures.

But the $900 savings and elapsed time differences aren't really the point. By requiring five people to approve the purchase order, the company created five opportunities for someone to make the wrong decision. Only Joe had knowledge or experience in furnace operations! "This told me two things," Joe said. "One, they're not very serious about keeping this place warm in the winter. Two, they don't trust me with $300."

Sometimes policies and procedures seem to serve no useful purpose other than to give Scott Adams material for his "Dilbert" comic strip or to make company leaders look like they don't have any sense.

Consider Cheryl. Cheryl became manager of public affairs at a large insurance company. On her first day on the job, her new supervisor showed her to her office. A few maintenance folks were moving furniture and wastebaskets in and out of the room. In the corner stood a representative from human resources.

"Your office is a director's office," the HR rep said. "We need to change a few things so that it will comply with policies for a manager's office."

Wooden wastebaskets went out. Metal ones came in. Fabric covered chairs came in. Leather covered chairs went out.

When the job seemed finished, the HR rep announced that the maintenance crew now needed to tape the curtains shut. "We need to tape them so they can't be opened," the HR rep announced. "A director's office has a window, but a manager's office doesn't. Since you're only a manager, you aren't supposed to be able to look out the window." (For those who haven't been exposed to such bureaucratic absurdities, I assure you this is a true story.)

The new communications manager told me, "How absurd. I'm a manager, so I can't look out a window? It made me think of my kids in the backseat of our family car. 'Hey, Mother, Johnny's looking out my window. Tell him to stop it.'

"I stayed there two days. Their communication was clear. They didn't want adults working for them. They wanted children."

One of the best business policies is business casual every day, and one of the worst is business casual only on Friday. While Letitia Baldrige, corporate manners guru-manqué, refers to casual business dress as the "slobbing of America," casual business dress is here and probably isn't going away anytime soon. It promotes comfort and informality, which can contribute to candor and openness. According to a Levi-Strauss & Company survey, more than half of the office workers in the United States dress casually every day. That's up 22 percent since 1995.[12]

But for one of the goofiest policies, consider casual Friday. It goes something like this. We want to impress the customer, so we need to wear business attire. But since other companies are relaxing their dress codes, we'll nod in that direction and "give employees something they want." So Monday through Thursday, we'll wear business dress, and on Friday we'll dress down to business casual.

How is the customer any different on Friday than he is on Monday through Thursday? Do we dress for the customer or don't we?

When we relax dress on Friday, are we relaxing our commitment to the customer by 20 percent? Mixed messages!

Engaged people have a lot of flexibility to act. When the dots connect, when people think and act like business owners, they'll know which rules to follow, which rules to ignore, and which rules to change. They'll use good judgment. They'll dress right because it's in their best interest to do so.

Resource Allocation

Show me the money!

You can tell someone all day long that you support his or her line of business. But withholding funds needed to make that business grow communicates an entirely different story. (If you withhold needed money because there *is* no money available to allocate, you should communicate this to your people or they'll end up hearing a different message—that you don't support their business.)

The chairman of a railroad client was simultaneously communicating to employees that safety was paramount and that the company needed to cut costs dramatically in order to compete more effectively with the trucking industry. But when an employee in the railroad yard saw cutbacks that affected safety, he was confused. "Hey, which is really important here?" he asked. "I hear both are important, but it seems to me that cutting costs is *really* more important than my safety."

An airline told its flight attendants that customer satisfaction was critical to the company's ability to compete. In an effort to hold down costs, however, the company often ordered fewer meals than there were passengers on the planes. "They're telling us that costs are more important than the customers, pure and simple," one flight attendant told me.

A services firm told its people they needed to help improve profitability, yet refused to share basic financial information to guide employee decision-making. That is the equivalent of telling a sports team to go out and win, while neglecting to tell the players the game's rules and prohibiting them from looking at the scoreboard.

A consumer products company told its research and development people that the company needed to get more new products into the pipeline, as they say in the R&D world. But for cost reasons, the company denied R&D's requests to travel to meet with brand managers and sales people, who knew firsthand what new products customers wanted. When the decision was later reversed, brand managers and sales people began meeting regularly with the R&D people, and the company began to dramatically improve its new product introduction record.

Providing people with the technology they need to do their jobs communicates. Withholding it does too. I was staying at a hotel a few years ago and before turning in, I called the operator to request a wake-up call. She asked what time I wanted to be awakened, and I told her 6 a.m. "I'm sorry," the operator said, "but that will be impossible. All of our 6 a.m. slots are taken. We can call you at 5:30 or 6:30." She proceeded to tell me that the hotel had only a limited number of people who could be awakened by the hotel's wake-up service at any given time. "If you insist on getting up when you say you need to get up," she explained, "you'll need to use the alarm clock we've provided in your room." Although I was aghast, think what she must really have thought when her general manager lectured about being customer-focused.

Working Environment

Your customers are just like you. They form first impressions of a store, plant, office, or agency when they drive into the parking lot. They form second impressions when they walk up to your front door, third impressions when they encounter your receptionist, and fourth impressions if they ever get beyond the receptionist.

So do your people, except they form the first four impressions and then dozens of others when you're recruiting them and after they come to work day after day. Just as your customers are bombarded with environmental cues about your business when they walk up to your front door, your people receive a continuous and much more intimate dose of environmental cues every day.

Working environment increasingly is becoming a way companies can differentiate themselves to people they're recruiting. Today's younger workers are looking for challenge, excitement, and fun, along with a sense of personal pride and satisfaction. "A cool place to work." Your work environment can communicate a lot about you and your values. All other things equal, it could be what turns on or turns off that super recruit with hot skills.

Remember how the Owens Corning employees were intimidated by the special floor and its high ceilings, deep carpet, pricey artwork, and lack of observable workers? There was no sign outside the 28th floor elevators saying: AVERAGE RUN-OF-THE-MILL EMPLOY-EES CAN'T COME ONTO THE 28TH FLOOR! Or UNLESS YOU'RE VICE-PRESIDENT OR ABOVE, TURN BACK NOW! It was the environment itself that communicated that "average" employees weren't welcome. In actuality, they may well have been welcomed, but the environment communicated otherwise.

A former colleague, Richard Bevan, recently visited a company in the U.K. "There was a suite of well-protected offices for directors," he tells me. "The offices were marked DIRECTORS: PRIVATE. I pointed out the negative message to them. Three weeks later, when I visited, they had a new sign. It just read PRIVATE."

Many business leaders don't understand the importance of using environment to communicate. Their naiveté often is first manifested on that so-called executive floor, a term I dislike because of its connotation of hierarchy. There are still business leaders who think their carpet must be thicker than other people's carpets. There are still business leaders who think they're impressing someone with those doleful sentinels sitting outside their offices who act as guard dogs, ready to pounce on and deny entrance to anyone who's not "worthy." (There are still some sentinels who introduce themselves as Ms. Tightash rather than using their first names.)

What does this kind of environment communicate? Here's what I hear from employees, and what they would tell anyone who preserves this sort of hierarchic nonsense, only if they could get the chance. You're aloof. You're out of touch. You're detached. You think you're better than everyone else.

People know. They read the same papers and watch the CNN that you do. They've seen CEOs everywhere take the big dive: Agee, Akers, Allen, Lorenzo, Pfeiffer, Smithburg, Stempel, Whitmore, Lego, Dunlap, Erickson, you get the drift. They know leaders are like anyone else but just don't know it... yet.

Business leaders may have been able to get away with this in a different environment. But today, people want to know that their leaders are in tune, in touch, accessible. They've seen far too many layoffs that were caused by poor leadership, by leaders who were out of touch and didn't understand how to run their companies in the new business environment and now in the new economy. Leaders today need to continually earn the respect of the people they're leading. If they don't, they're apt not to keep leading them. Someone's going to leave, either the leader or those she or he is trying to lead.

Working environments are communication tools. When the health care company Manor Care moved its offices from one Washington, D.C., suburb to another, its leadership team was determined to use the opportunity to create an open, team-based environment. Its new "offices" have very few offices. Most people sit in cubicles, and there are few barriers among them. There are a lot of conference rooms and team rooms where people can conduct impromptu meetings. Larry Diamond, director of facilities services for Manor Care, says the objective is accessibility. "The important thing we did was open up communication," Diamond says.

Just as your office working environment communicates, so do the working environments in all the other offices and plants in the business.

When people come into your organization, their eyes and minds are working a thousand miles a minute. Walking through your maze of offices and corridors and out into your assembly plants, they're learning a lot about you and your organization from what the environment communicates. They see a lot of what employees see.

So what are they seeing in your place?

> Bright, clean, modern team rooms and communication centers out in the plant where people gather, get the news, problem-solve, and go online for information? Or dirty, dingy, smelly breakrooms cluttered with meaningless wall hangings, dented soda machines, and rickety furniture?

> Bulletin boards with nothing more than an outdated EEO policy and a yellowed OSHA poster? Or bulletin boards with today's cost and quality scores?

> Pallets that look as though they've been stacked using a carpenter's plumb bob? Or sloppily stacked finished goods that pose safety threats?

> Carefully drawn and recently repainted yellow lines delineating pedestrian walkways from forklift corridors? Or people dangerously going every which way out in the warehouse?

> Empty shelves? Full shelves?

> Open offices? Closed doors?

> Quiet offices with no signs of life? Or rowdy offices where people are having fun?

> Personalized workspaces with family and pet pictures and Gary Larson cartoons? Or dull, sterile offices with Dilbert cartoons?

When a machine spits out a flawed part, do they see people toss it aside, and keep working, or do they see flipcharts, root cause analysis, active problem-solving efforts, and a kaizen team kick in?

Bored looking people? Or teams celebrating with high fives?

Dark, mournful plants that are hot in the summer and cold in the winter? Or brightly lighted, freshly painted plants that maintain a constant 72 degrees?

Systems *do* speak. The five systems described in this chapter are the parts of the infrastructure people watch most. Others are powerful, too, however. They include how you make decisions; how you recruit, staff, and orient people; and how you outsource, provide employee benefits, create new products, manage technology, and sell and distribute your products and services. Every system in your infrastructure communicates. Neglected or ignored systems can wreak havoc on the organization when they conflict with other messages that are needed to drive decision moments and discretionary effort— when they're needed to connect the dots.

CHAPTER 6

The Power of Huddles and Channels

Our policy is to tell the whole truth and as little of it as possible.

— Anonymous railroad company leader

Formal communication channels represent the third communication source in any business (Figure 6-1). These include all printed, audiovisual, and Web-based communication, as well as the meetings that occur throughout our businesses. It's the formal way that we communicate, from memos, e-mail, voicemail, suggestion programs, business television, training sessions, newsletters, magazines, message boards, and bulletin boards to videos, postcards, teasers, banners, posters, paycheck inserts, kiosks, leader packets, audiocassettes, the Internet, and your intranet.

Formal communication media offer considerable value. They can provide context by keeping people updated on the business environment, customer expectations, and competitor and regulatory activity that influences the company and what it's trying to achieve. Sears'

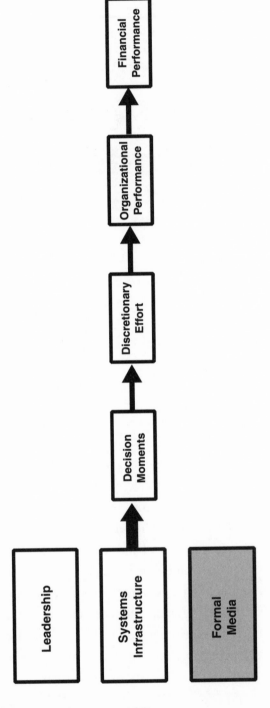

Figure 6-1. Communication source three.

S Journal and *S Update* are good examples of formal media that work well at that.

Formal media can reinforce the company's vision and strategy. They can celebrate and recognize people for actions that are consistent with the behavior an organization is trying to encourage. Hallmark Cards' *Noon News*, for example, comes out every day. It's filled with stories that recognize people for doing things in a way that is consistent with what Hallmark needs to continue its success.

Formal media can explain in detail new and changing human resource strategies and plans. AT&T, Southwest Airlines, and Kimberly-Clark, among others, do this well.

Voicemail can speed information around the world to people in far-flung locations or to project team members who telecommute or can't meet every time they have to exchange information.

Web-technology. The Internet and intranets. What fantastic creatures we've created. There's so much good about them.

Web technology has helped pry open a lot of businesses that have kept their people in the dark for years. When properly used it, coupled with e-mail, has done more to open communication in business than any other single medium or channel. With the Web, it is hard to keep a secret. People in chat rooms can analyze new product development information before the head of R&D even gets the information. Mergers and acquisitions can be the subject of Web-talk rumors before the leadership team knows the details of the deal.

For companies that have historically shared vast amounts of information in order to improve performance, Web-based technology has given them a turbo-boost. It's a communication channel that can push and pull information at twitch speed. It gives people access to personal portals which, in turn, help them customize information to their needs. It gives sales people the ability to beam customer orders into distribution centers so customers can get their goods in a fraction of the time that it took before. It gives a sense of connectedness to people operating in remote parts of the world.

Networked computers have penetrated to the factory floor and are in the offices. They help people call up current product specifications, order replacement parts, review current manufacturing processes, and engage in dialogue with other employees around the world. Motorola is using intranets to improve product development and introduction times. They used a factory-based intranet to help their Mansfield, Massachusetts plant roll out new cable modems within six weeks. This eliminated costly start-up costs, made elaborate training unnecessary and enabled workers to quickly identify not only new parts and instructions but also production steps that had high error rates.

Hewlett-Packard has put nearly all information to its people on the internal web. "In fact," Lew Platt, HP's chairman says, "we've been able to take information sharing to the point where we've achieved a measurable increase in productivity. In the past few years alone, our computer systems sales reps have seen their sales quotas increase five-fold, while their selling cost envelope has been cut in half."[13]

The wonderful world of Web-technology. It facilitates speed, improve quality and service, lowers costs and enhances innovation.

But, too much of anything can be, well, too much. We must keep in mind that Web-technology isn't an end unto itself, that it's part of a larger communication system that needs to be managed.

I readily admit to being somewhat drawn to technological toys. I was an early user of cell phones, back when they weighed a ton and would barely fit into a briefcase. I was an early owner of Global Positioning System (GPS), a nifty satellite triangulation gizmo that tells me within a few feet where I am in my sailboat on the Chesapeake Bay. But GPS in all its technological glory won't sail the sailboat. Close, but not quite. There are many other sailing system components that need to be managed as well to sail a sailboat effectively and efficiently.

This is also true with Web-technology. Remarkable as it is, there are many other communication system components that need to be managed as well in order to drive a business forward.

When I got my first GPS, I confess to becoming transfixed by it even on sunny days in waters in which I'd been sailing for 20 years, sometimes only a few miles from home port. As I eventually learned all that it could do for me, as well as its limitations, my near obsession with GPS subsided. Today, I'm much more realistic about its capabilities.

We need to treat Web-technology the same way. We need to continue to learn about it and learn from it, and then apply this technology in ways that will best help our businesses. We also must appreciate that Web-technology is only one piece of a much larger communication system.

We must carefully balance high-tech and high-touch communication.

People today are no different than they were 10 years ago, before the Web. They want relevant business information to help them perform better. Often that's best delivered via the Web. Yet, they need the high touch afforded by one-on-one and team meetings, chance hallway discussions and high fives when projects go well.

At the beginning of 2000, I led a team that assessed communication inside a global technology company. More than 90 percent of the company's employees said they preferred to receive business-related information online versus on paper, when given that choice. But, when asked to assess the *importance* of 16 communication channels that existed in the company, one-on-one meetings scored highest followed by staff meetings and then the corporate intranet. These three communication channels were, in employees' eyes, *equally effective*. Remember that this was in a company where people tend to be more technologically oriented.

Technology companies may be especially prone to over-emphasizing high tech at the expense of high touch. I've spoken with call center employees (These are the people you reach when you call for technical assistance.) who say they never see or talk to their supervisors, managers, or anyone else in leadership positions. As one told me: "She's [his supervisor] an engineer who's much more comfortable sending me e-mails than having meetings." I've met with employees inside one of the world's greatest technology labs and have heard them complain about the lack of face-to-face communication from what they referred to as "an aloof, distant, and disconnected management."

We need to get every last drop of good from technology, but we need to manage technology as part of an integrated communication system in order to deliver what people truly need—high tech and high touch.

Working together, all of the formal communication channels can have an immense impact on a business. But their true potential can only be realized when they're working in tandem with the other two communication sources—leadership and the systems infrastructure. Yet all too often business leaders try to use the formal communication media exclusively to perform a communication job that the formal media can't do alone, such as communicating change.

Professor John Kotter of Harvard says he's seen three patterns with respect to using formal communication media to communicate change. "In the first, a group actually does develop a pretty good transformation vision and then proceeds to communicate it by holding a single meeting or sending out a single communication. Having used about .0001 percent of the yearly intracompany communication capability, the group is startled that few people seem to understand the new approach."

Concerning the second approach, Kotter goes on to say, "The head of the organization spends a considerable amount of time making speeches to employee groups, but most people still don't get it" (not surprising, since vision captures only .0005 percent of the total yearly communication).

"In the third pattern, much more effort goes into newsletters and speeches, but some very visible senior executives still behave in ways that are antithetical to the vision. The net result is that cynicism among the troops goes up, while belief in communication goes down. Without credible communication, and a lot of it, the hearts and minds of the troops are never captured."[14]

Figure 6-2 shows the results of a say/do assessment at a large company. Employees were asked the extent to which the company's leadership said certain values were important and the extent to which the company actually acted on the values. The dark bars on the left represent the "say" score and the light bars on the right represent the "do" score. As you can see, there are sizable say/do gaps. This is not unusual when an organization is going through significant change, as is this company. However, there is danger in allowing the "say communication" to get too far ahead of the "do communication." The principal concern, of course, should be the leadership's credibility. How

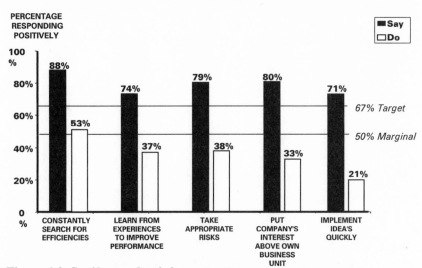

Figure 6-2. Say/do on what is important to company success.

much talk will your people tolerate without seeing the corresponding walk? At what point do they turn off? At what point will performance decline? At what point will they leave? At what point will it be difficult for you to attract top performers?

In a meeting with a group of employees in a global retail company, one of the employees said: "I read the company publication, but when you come down to it, it just isn't that believable. It would have you believe that everything is wonderful. The president is kind of a good news guy so he wants [the publication] to have only good news in it. But either [the publication] is out of touch or he's out of touch. Someday, I'd like him to come down here and come into our department and see how life really is in this company. It creates a real credibility problem for him."

Another group of employees in a large mass-merchandise company was telling me about a new continuous improvement effort that the CEO had launched about six months prior to my meeting with them. Employees related that they'd read and heard all about the initiative in the various employee publications and during meetings with top management. "But I can tell you it's not happening," one employee said. "He [the CEO] thinks we're all doing this continuous improvement stuff, but we're not. In my department it's business as usual," the employee said. "Top management is out of touch with what's really going on in this company."

The CEO of a noted insurance company experienced say/do gaps. He and his leadership team conducted a companywide video conference in which the company's leaders outlined six strategic objectives. The CEO made it clear that the company was serious about the six objectives and that people would be seeing a lot of activities in the coming months designed to achieve them. A few weeks after the conference, the company distributed cards that listed the six objectives. Employees were supposed to tuck the little cards in their wallets, lest they forget what the objectives were. (Cards with the six objectives on them represented gimmickry more than substance. I've never known anyone who changed their behavior as a result of being handed a wallet card adorned with lofty objectives.)

Three months after the video conference, my colleagues and I conducted a series of focus group discussions with employees to assess the communication environment, especially around the six strategic objectives. Many people were able to tell us the subject matter of the objectives (e.g., growth and profit), but they understood little else, including how much growth or how much profit or the contribution they were supposed to make to growth or profit. They'd received no additional information after the video conference about the objectives other than the wallet-sized cards. It was the equivalent of telling a sports team that their objective is to win but neglecting to tell them what game they are playing. Soccer? Baseball? Football? Or you could liken it to telling the Chicago Symphony to play well but neglecting to hand out the music score. Bach? Brahms? Bizet?

The credibility of the CEO and his leadership team was tarnished.

Aside from Web-based technology, e-mail, and voicemail, much of the formal communication media suffer from two maladies. They don't get information to people when they need it, largely because of elaborate approval processes. And they aren't operationally relevant, that is, their content has little to do with improving business performance.

Once, as part of a communication assessment, I needed to evaluate an electric power company's employee publication. The publication's cycle time was so long that the holiday issue came out in March. Another issue carried word of an employee's death and marriage, both in the same issue. (I've forgotten which appeared first.)

Recently, I reviewed a 16-page employee newspaper from a well-regarded Fortune 100 company. Ten of the newspaper's 16 pages were filled with real estate ads, want ads, and display ads for jewelers, carpet centers, banks, restaurants, and a couple of local car dealerships.

There was a crossword puzzle and some social club announcements. There was a front-page story about a board meeting that could have been written three weeks before the meeting. There was nothing in the article of any value to anyone.

One story talked about career paths and another recognized some employees for technical excellence. These were the only two stories that employees could act on. The career path story helped people understand a process they could use to examine and manage their own careers. The recognition story communicated one of the company's important values—technical excellence—and indirectly communicated that doing what the people who were recognized did is what the company would like many of its other employees to do.

What must shareholders say about this use of company money and time? Do customers benefit from this investment? Does anyone?

More to the point, perhaps: Is this publication typical? Certainly not every employee publication is crammed with this much advertising. But the publication *is* typical in its lack of operational relevance. It's also typical of employee publications in that it provides little information to help people improve the business.

Contrast these kinds of publications with formal communication channels that provide people with *forecasts* that they can use to influence the business. Consider the case of a multidiscipline team at a manufacturing company. The team began the meeting I attended by distributing a document that reported a potential negative inventory variance two months out. In other words, if nothing were done, the company would have more inventory in its warehouse than it had planned at the beginning of the year. Excess inventory would affect the bottom line and their bonuses. Two people in the meeting were sales people. Each identified customers who would be willing to take the excess inventory off the company's hands. The negative variance was thus avoided.

Here, an operationally relevant publication helped avoid a problem. A traditional publication, such as the one described above, would have waited to report that "last month the company experienced a negative 15 percent inventory variance." This news would have helped no one improve the business. This news lacks operational relevance.

One formal communication process stands out above all others for its ability to link people to strategy and connect the dots. It's called huddling. *Huddling is not a single formal communication medium. It is a process that combines and integrates several formal communication media to improve performance.*

I first observed huddling during a consulting project I conducted for Mars, Inc., the food products company known for its M&M and Mars candies, Kal-Kan dog food, and Uncle Ben's rice.

Mars always has been known as highly secretive with the outside world. But inside the company, Mars moves a lot of information quickly and accurately. Mars associates, as they call themselves, pride themselves on their open environments—no offices and glassed conference rooms. The company's leaders, John and Forrest Mars, sit at their desks, out in the open, with other Mars associates at the company's McLean, Virginia, corporate headquarters.

There are formal meetings at Mars, but there's even more informal give and take, chance hallway conversations and quick informal standup meetings. People come together quickly, agree on a course of action quickly, disband, and act quickly.

Mars doesn't call these meetings huddles, but that's what they're like. After watching them operate for a couple of months, I realized that they were huddling quickly, just as U.S. football teams huddle quickly and then run the next play.

Ritz-Carlton Hotels uses a more structured form of huddles.

At 9 a.m. every day, the company's 80 top managers gather for a 10-minute standup meeting in the hallway outside the office of the president and COO, Horst Schultz. Within 24 hours, the rest of the company's employees will also have met on similar subjects at their daily shift meetings.

According to Leonardo Inghilleri, senior vice president of human resources there, "The meeting is part training, part operations, part philosophy—all conducted with drill-like efficiency. We work in a 7-days-a-week, 24-hours-a-day business, and our customers are diverse. Employees need to know how to think on their feet to solve a problem.

"We prepare a monthly calendar of lineup topics—ranging from the opening of a new hotel in Dubai to meeting-planner programs— and e-mail them weekly to each hotel. For one critical moment every day," Inghilleri says, "the entire organization is aligned behind the same issue."

Inghilleri explains that the meeting has three parts. "First, we introduce the topic of the week. Second, we revisit one of our customer service basics. Finally, we run through operational issues that are specific to each department, anything from the specials on the menu to an upcoming meeting with an investor. Ten minutes after the meeting begins, everyone is back at work."[15]

The open-book management concept fosters an even more disciplined approach to huddling.

In his excellent book on the subject, *The Open-Book Experience*, John Case describes huddling as "a structured series of meetings designed specifically to allow people to participate in running the business."

Huddling is a high-involvement communication process, where the focal point is the performance scorecard. In open-book companies, huddles are disciplined, quick, to-the-point, data-driven, and filled with stories about people and what they do, how they won by hitting their targets, and what help they need to hit future targets.

The huddling process open-book style is really a rigorous *cycle* of meetings. Figure 6-3 depicts that cycle. But don't confuse them with

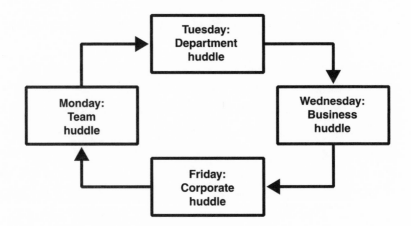

Figure 6-3. The huddling process.

the old run-of-the-mill team or department meetings that occur in most organizations. Huddling is differentiated in part by its rigor. John Case explains further:

> Each week every business unit holds a meeting to review its performance for the past week. Department representatives arrive with key numbers in hand and report them at the meeting. Typically, the numbers are entered into a computer spreadsheet, and the spreadsheet is projected onto a screen so that everybody there can see it. In effect, a rudimentary income statement is created on the spot. But attendees are not merely examining last week's raw numbers; they're also reporting how they did compared to plan and discussing any variances that seem worth discussing. In addition, they're offering opinions as to what lies ahead, for the rest of the current month, at least, and often out into the next month or two. The spreadsheet shows three numbers for every line item: actual, plan, and opinion.
>
> At the end of the meeting, the financial report is printed out and distributed. Departmental reps—usually, but not always, the department manager—take them back for a posthuddle with ev-

eryone in the department. How are we doing in addressing these variances? What needs to be done to get ready for the rest of this month and for the next month? Before the next huddle, a department may get together to report and examine its internal numbers (a prehuddle). People know that at the huddles they'll be expected to explain variances and have action plans at the ready. They know that they'll be accountable not only for the numbers but also for how the department (like any business) is preparing itself for the future.

"When we come out of the meeting," says open-book pioneer Jack Stack of Springfield ReManufacturing, "we can see the whole field before us. We know who is where, how the game is unfolding, and what each of us has to do to make sure we keep moving closer to the goal line."

The huddling system is quite simple. It's merely a back-and-forth cycle of structured meetings devoted to how the business is running and focused primarily on budgets and forecasts. In open-book companies, the primary formal media used in the huddles are the income and cash flow statements. They can be disseminated through an intranet or in printed form.

Huddle timeframes and agendas vary, depending on the needs of each specific company. Nevertheless, let's take a look at a typical huddling process. Let's assume that our hypothetical process begins with a department huddle on Monday. Let's also assume that there are two levels in the organization. (If your organization has more than two levels, as most large companies do, just add another huddle for each level.)

Monday: Department Huddle

People in each department assemble, compare last month's actuals with forecasts, and draw some conclusions about the results. Then they develop forecasts and discuss any important information behind the numbers for the current month and next month. Where forecasts appear to be favorable compared to plan, the huddle identifies any steps that need to be taken to make sure the numbers end up favorably. Where forecasts are unfavorable (i.e., there's a projected negative variance in the numbers, such as an inventory variance), the huddle attempts to identify steps that can be taken to get back on track. Here are some questions people in the huddle might ask:

- What are the biggest threats to achieving forecast?
- Do we have opportunities to come in better than forecast?
- Given the issues, what actions should we commit to?
- Should we modify our forecast in light of our conclusions?

Members of the huddle address other relevant issues, consolidate the numbers for the business unit huddle, and usually engage in what some call roundtable news. Roundtable news is just that—a discussion of any other events or activities that the department members should be aware of, as well as recognition or celebrations for such successes as winning a new contract or finding a way to fix a defect-producing machine.

Huddle members then consolidate their numbers and develop the core messages or story that one of its members will take to the business unit huddle.

Elapsed time: One hour

Tuesday: Business Unit Huddle

Most companies that use the huddling process require that someone from each department be represented at the business unit huddle. In some companies, the representative is the department manager, supervisor, or team leader. In others, it's whoever the department might send, based on availability. For example, a department might send someone who would benefit from business unit huddle exposure; it can be an excellent professional development opportunity.

The business unit huddle's agenda is the same as that for the department huddle, but the business unit huddle focuses on more aggregated numbers. That is, whereas the department huddle concentrated on department numbers, the business unit huddle focuses on business unit numbers. Business unit huddles consolidate their numbers and identify core messages they want to send to the corporate, or main huddle.

Elapsed time: One hour

Wednesday: Corporate, or Main Huddle

Business unit representatives (typically the heads of the business units) come together at the corporate huddle, sometimes called a main huddle. They use an agenda similar to that used by the department and business unit huddles, except now the numbers have been further aggregated to the corporate or company level. Participants review last month's forecasts and actual numbers as well as year-to-date numbers, as did those attending the department and business unit huddles. Then they focus their attention on the current month and next month to identify opportunities to reinforce success or to avoid negative variances in the plan.

Corporate business leaders often use their huddles to look beyond a few months, perhaps out as far as the remainder of the year.

They also develop core messages for posthuddles or for 10- to 20-minute business unit and department huddles that will take place over the next 24 hours. As they identify core messages, they might consider the following questions:

- What's important to communicate?
- How do we reinforce the focused message or story?

- What do we want people to focus on?
- What action do we want people to take?
- Do we have special messages for any special group?

Revised forecasts are updated at the meeting. Notes are kept by a meeting participant so business unit participants can share consistent information with the rest of their business units and, in turn, with departments in the business units.

Elapsed time: One hour

Thursday: Posthuddles

Business unit huddle participants next meet for 10 to 20 minutes with department representatives to review corporate or main huddle scorecards, forecasts, and notes on key messages that need to be communicated throughout the departments. They use these meetings to discuss any action that needs to be taken to improve results or avoid shortfalls. Department representatives use this day and the next to communicate with their people in each department.

Elapsed time: 10–20 minutes each for the business unit and department posthuddles.

As you can see, this entire process requires less than four hours of the company's time. The most time any one person devotes to the process is about two and a half hours. This four-hour investment of company time in a rich communication process makes it possible for *everyone* in a company to have information about subjects such as:

- Where they are against plan for the year
- How they'll do this month
- Forecasts for the next month or so

- What action they need to take to ensure positive results and to avoid negative results in the future
- What actions others are taking
- Who got recognized for a positive contribution to the company

How many company employees do you know who have this kind of detailed information? The huddles help make this happen.

Some business leaders might say: "That all sounds great, but we're about meetinged out. We don't have time for another bunch of meetings." Well, the huddling process replaces many other meetings, especially the unproductive ones many people complain about. Companies shouldn't "install" the huddling process on top of everything else they're doing to manage communication. Huddling can form the core of the company's formal communication process. It then can be supplemented with other meetings that might be necessary to running the business.

Others might say, "Yes, it sounds good, but we're a large, farflung company. We can't afford to have all these people shuttling back and forth to meetings." That's where e-mail, voicemail, video conferences, teleconferences, and the intranet can come into play. There's no one best approach to huddling. It has to work for you and your business.

Huddling is disciplined. It's rigorous, fast, relevant, and focused on improving performance. It epitomizes communication as a process rather than as a series of events and activities, whether connected or disconnected. It makes obsolete a lot of the discussion regarding supervisors as primary communicators and suggestion programs.

Integrated with leadership and infrastructure communication, huddling is a powerful communication process to use to connect the dots. It capitalizes fully on the use of technology to gather and disseminate information. Huddling can represent an excellent blend of high-tech and high-touch.

The huddling process should serve as a model for all formal com-

> There's the myth that people want information primarily from their supervisors. No study ever reported this. It is true that people want certain information from supervisors—information about team goals, performance feedback, and pay, for instance. But, people want information from other sources as well. We want corporate vision, direction, and strategy from leadership. We want project information from teammates. We want new product ideas from our customers. We want a lot of information from e-mail, voicemail, and online sources. Some recent research is revealing that people increasingly prefer information delivered to them online rather than on paper or from their supervisor. Is there a role for the supervisor? Yes, of course. But the supervisor shouldn't be the ultimate pivot point for all information dissemination in today's speed- and cost-driven world.

munication media. When designed and implemented well, it can achieve real business performance improvements.

The formal communication media have a job to do and they're often good at it. But they're also often called on to perform jobs they weren't designed to perform. Why, for instance, do companies try to use a video as the main communication source of a major change message? Why do they try to connect people to the business strategy with one meeting? It's like trying to dig a hole with a hammer. Is it because it's easy? It probably is easier to "get a memo out" or "put out another video" than it is to shift leadership behavior or align the systems infrastructure and the messages it sends.

Although it may be easy, sometimes it's wrong. This stuff is hard work.

CHAPTER 7

Linking People to Strategy

*You need to communicate to get information.
You need to communicate to get cooperation.
You need to communicate to let others know
what you're doing. You need to communicate
to get feedback. You need to communicate
because few people live in isolation. You need
to communicate because human beings are
social creatures.*

— Edward de Bono, author, scholar

I magine you've been invited to your neighbor's house on a Saturday night to play a team-oriented board game with several other
neighbors. The game is new to you. Logically, you want to know
a few things before you begin, like the game's objectives and the best
tactics to deploy to win. You want to know what *you* need to do to
help your team, what knowledge or skills are required to defeat your
opponents, and what's at stake for the winners and the losers.

The information you need to know to play the game successfully
is no different than the information you and anyone else need to win

in business. Companies that link people to their strategy share intense amounts of information that people need, not just to participate but to become passionately engaged in the game of winning.

"Need to know" is an old expression with military overtones. Autocratic organizations that run along the lines of a strict command-and-control hierarchy often speak of providing information on a "need to know" basis. Managers, like officers in the army, decide what people need to know. Then they sprinkle crumbs of information to the workers—the troops—giving out no more than is absolutely necessary for people to do their jobs as they're told to do them. When managers operate on a need to know basis, employees operate in a *need to do* mode. They do no more than is absolutely necessary to do their jobs and go home. People have perfected the art of looking like they're working.

Businesses that link people to the business share information in a way that captures as much discretionary effort as they can from the people in the organization. People respond by giving more than what's absolutely necessary. They do what it takes to win.

In these organizations, it's not "management" that decides what people need to know. It's the people doing the work who decide what *they* need to know in order to achieve their goals and the goals of the business. When they don't get the information they need, they're apt to rebel, because they're on the line to deliver. There are consequences to them and the business when they don't deliver. Some call this "demand-pull communication."

Leaders are responsible for making sure their people have the information needed to win. If leaders don't do this, they're not doing their jobs.

So what do we need to know to win?

To win at business, we need to connect the dots. To connect the dots, we need the same basic information we need when we go to our neighbors to play that board game that's new to us. We need five categories of information, as shown in the first column of Figure 7-1.

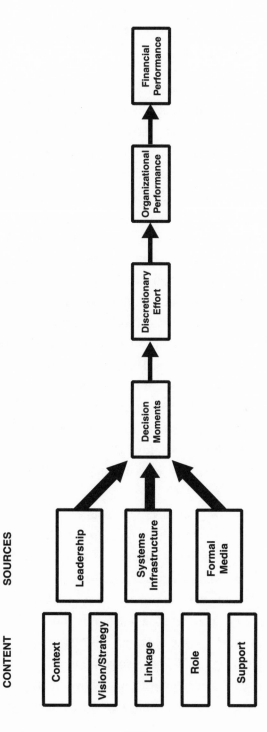

CONTENT

SOURCES

Context

Vision/Strategy

Linkage

Role

Support

Leadership

Systems Infrastructure

Formal Media

Decision Moments

Discretionary Effort

Organizational Performance

Financial Performance

Figure 7-1.

Context

Context is the beginning of line of sight. It gives us perspective. It explains "why." It helps make sense of everything else. Superior leaders are able to take everything that's happening around them and develop an elegant, powerful perspective and interpretation that captures hearts and minds. Context is the foundation for change. It gives people a reason. Without it, people lack an argument for doing things differently.

On one particular assignment, I was interviewing a group of telephone company employees in Florida. They were lamenting the company's seeming lack of direction. They described their frustration over the mixed messages their company was sending. One minute they were supposed to do one thing, the next minute, another.

"First thing yesterday, I go off to empowerment training," a lineman told me. "I learn how to be empowered. Then they send me over to learn how to solve problems. Then I go to a safety meeting. Then I do something called team-based management. In between, I'm getting messages from my supervisor telling me two different things are priorities. At about four o'clock, I go out to my truck to start to do some real work with what's left of the day. Then I think to myself: Would someone please make sense out of all this? Does anybody know what's going on here?"

Would someone please make sense out of all this?

That's a question we're all asking. For the telephone lineman and today's CEOs, the world has turned upside down. This morning's competitors are this afternoon's customers. Today we merge. Tomorrow we downsize. We acquire a company because of its perfect fit on one day, then spin it off later because it's "not within our core business."

How can we make sense out of all this? By creating an intelligent and relevant framework. "Give us some context!"

People in nearly every industry know that change is with us now and forever. They know that things aren't as neat and tidy as they once were. Things are changing daily, so they want perspective: on how the business works, on what the new rules are, on what customers really want and don't want, and on who the competitors are and what they're trying to do to beat us. Just as we want to know the unfamiliar board game's objectives, we want to know the objectives of the business, what it takes to win.

The need for context isn't confined to so-called frontline employees. Many business leaders are as unsure of the context of their businesses as anyone else is. Some of it might be understandable, given the speed and magnitude of change. But some of that is unnecessary. Many leaders haven't performed the basic research or conducted the rigorous analysis needed to uncover the drivers of their businesses. If leadership doesn't know what drives their businesses, they can't communicate those drivers. And if they can't communicate the drivers, how can they expect their people to understand the rules of the game and what it takes to win?

The leader of a financial institution posed this interesting question: How, in today's technology-driven world, do you prevent employees from hearing news about their companies from the news media first? "With everything so open, and with information moving so fast, how can you keep your employees from being ambushed on the

---

I remember once getting into a discussion with the chairman of a global chemical company on ways to improve communication management. With a twinkle in his eye and a tongue in his cheek, he said, "You know, Jim, it was a lot simpler in the old days, when you could just tell people things and they'd just accept it. You don't suppose the pendulum will ever swing back to those days, do you?"

I responded that I suspected the pendulum could swing back if we could find a way of preventing everyone in the organization from watching CNN when they went home at night and got up in the morning. "Otherwise," I said, "I doubt if the pendulum is going to swing back."

The pendulum *won't* swing back.

---

street by a reporter who has gotten hold of a major story about the company that the company didn't get the chance to communicate to its employees first?"

In the pre-online world, communicating news to employees (especially bad news) before they heard about it in the news media was a noble goal. It still is. However, today's chat rooms are making that goal increasingly unrealistic.

When people understand the context, accurate news about the company that a reporter could report would likely be met with a resounding "That makes sense."

When people understand context, they understand the big picture. They have a framework for managing decision moments and for managing what they do and don't do.

Context makes everything else make sense. It's the foundation for connecting people to strategy.

Vision and Strategy

A vision is a target, a picture of the future. A strategy is a roadmap, how you're going to achieve the vision.

Over the past decade, many business leaders have consumed a lot of time, energy, and money creating fancy vision statements. They've marched their leadership teams off-site for a few days and "wordsmithed" lofty phrases that in the aggregate read pretty much like everybody else's vision statement. Returning to their offices, they called in their public relations folks and directed that the new vision statement be printed on posters, pens, wallet cards, coffee mugs, ballpoint pens, pyramids, table tents, balloons, and anything else they could think of. Leadership then returned to business as usual, thinking they'd done their job. "We have a vision," they would proclaim, "and we've communicated it."

In *Built to Last,* James C. Collins and Jerry I. Porras address the myth of becoming a visionary company through vision statements.

> The visionary companies attained their stature not so much because they made visionary pronouncements. Nor did they rise to greatness because they wrote one of those vision, values, purpose, mission, or aspiration statements. Creating a statement can be a helpful *step* in building a visionary company, but it is only one of thousands of steps in a never-ending process of expressing the fundamental characteristics we identified across the visionary companies.

A vision needs to paint a clear picture of the future. After all, it is a *vision.* A vision helps people understand what the finished product is supposed to look like. A vision represents a behavioral portrait, so to speak. When we know what that portrait is supposed to look like when it's completed, we can better understand what we need to do, when we have decision moments and action options, to contribute to the finished portrait. Each action we take represents another brush stroke that's needed to create the vision.

Visions should be simple. Jack Welch focuses on "something big, but simple and understandable."

"Every idea you present must be something you could get across easily at a cocktail party with strangers," Welch says. "If only aficionados of your industry can understand what you're saying, you've blown it."

Vision and mission are related. A vision represents a destination. A mission represents an organization's purpose, why it exists. Many organizations have a strong sense of purpose, or mission. When their people connect to that mission, they connect to something greater than work. I've worked with that great team of people at the Mayo Clinic, based in Rochester, Minnesota. Everyone at Mayo knows the clinic's tripartite mission, which is focused on clinical practice, education, and research.

One hundred miles northwest of the Mayo Clinic is Medtronic, a $4 billion company that designs and manufacturers medical technology. Bill George is chairman and chief executive officer. "The subject of building a mission-driven and values-centered organization is near to my heart," George says. "I call this leadership with a purpose, meaning leadership with vision, passion, and compassion—vision of what our organization can become, passion for the people we serve, and compassion for the people with whom we work."

"I believe it starts with the basic reason we come to work every day. We want to serve others and help restore people to full life and health. We aren't there just for the money."

George advises his fellow CEOs to create written mission statements, but he warns against stopping with the words. "That's the easy part," he says. "The more difficult part is getting everyone to buy into that mission and those values. That takes time and effort and consistency of action, through bad times as well as good. It only takes one reversal of values at the top when conditions are tough to reverse many years of hard work in setting the standards and the climate. For better or worse, as leaders, we are better known for our deeds than for our words."[16]

Peter Drucker explains that today's knowledge workers need to be treated as volunteers.

> They have expectations, self-confidence, and above all, a network, and that gives them mobility, which is probably the greatest change in the human condition. A short time ago, if you were a peasant, you were going to stay a peasant. Even in this country [the U.S.], social mobility was almost unknown. Now, every young person I know has his or her résumé in the bottom drawer.
>
> So we have to treat almost everybody as a volunteer. They carry their tools in their heads and can go anywhere. And we

know what attracts and holds volunteers. The first thing is a clear mission.* People need to know what their organization stands for and is trying to accomplish.

Don't expect a 29-year-old or 33-year-old engineer to embrace a financial objective as a statement of mission. People want to know what their organization is here for and how they can contribute. It doesn't have to be anything high falutin', but it has to be concrete.[17]

An employee in an automobile assembly plant explained the difference between having a vision and not having a vision of the future. "It's like two of us trying to put together a 1000-piece puzzle," he said. "One of us has been shown a picture of the completed puzzle on the front of the box the puzzle came in. The other guy has no clue about what the puzzle is supposed to look like when it's finally put together. Which one will put the puzzle together first? Which one will be more productive? Which one will win? We spend most of our time around here just trying to figure out what top management has in mind—what their vision is. That's a waste of energy. Show us the front of the damned box and we'll put the puzzle together. Stop playing games with us."

An orchestra conductor in a smallish-sized town in the midwestern United States shows her orchestra members the "front of the box" *aurally*. If during their next performance the orchestra intends to play Dvorak's Symphony No. 9 "From the New World," she brings to the first rehearsal a compact disc of the Dvorak symphony as it was recorded by the Chicago Symphony Orchestra. After playing the CD, she says to the orchestra members, "When we sound like this, we'll invite the community to come hear us play." The orchestra rehearses and rehearses, pausing from time to time to relisten to the Chicago Symphony Orchestra at its finest. Each time the recording concludes,

---

*Drucker's use of the term *mission* corresponds to the term *vision* in this book: organizational purpose and the future state.

she repeats, "When we sound like this, we'll invite the community to come hear us play." And when she believes the orchestra members have the piece down as well as they'll ever get it down, she announces: "It's time to invite the community to come hear us play."

A vision! Every orchestra member hears what the final picture looks like. Every member, from the French horns to the violins to the clarinets to the tympani, has heard how his or her instrument fits into the vision and what it's supposed to sound like.

The leader's job is to communicate the vision, what "it" will look like when we get there, assuming that "there" is still there when we get there in this speed-driven world.

To realize the vision, we need a strategy, a plan for getting there. For the dots to connect, people need to know the strategy, at least the part that relates to them and what they do. I continue to be amazed by business leaders who don't think it's important to share their business strategy with the very people who have to implement that strategy. How many coaches of successful sports teams refuse to share the game plan with their players?

"It's as though they're saying, 'I have a plan to win. Now, you have to figure it out,'" an employee in a transportation company divulged. "Why play hide and seek with us? My guess is that if we knew the plan, we could implement it better than if we didn't." So-called frontline employees are smart that way!

But the voice of common sense doesn't always prevail.

Look at it this way: If you were betting on a game and everything was equal except that one team knew the game plan and one didn't, where would you put your money? You'd go with the informed team, of course. Everyone would, including your shareholders.

The Pepsi-Cola Company uses team meetings conducted by marketing unit managers across North America to explain the company's business and strategy. Employees gather around tables in groups of eight to discuss the strategy and what it means to them. They use learning maps, which graphically depict the business and its operating plan. In the discussions, employees are able to draw conclusions about the business and gain a better understanding of what is occurring in the industry and how the trends affect Pepsi. The first map, called Revolution on Beverage Street, traced the evolution of consumer needs and priorities and linked them with business trends and future implications. The second map, Street Fight, graphically depicted how consumer trends affected their customers' businesses. The third map, The Race is On, explained what competitors were doing and how well they were doing.[18]

How much strategy information should you share? If the purpose of sharing information is to provide people with what they need to improve performance, then you need to provide whatever information will help them do that. Different people and groups of people need different information about the strategy. The operative term is *relevance*, relevance to improving performance. For example, some of what's relevant to some people in the aerospace division of a company could also be relevant to some people in its automotive parts division. However, information relevant to one division might be irrelevant to another.

Do people working increasingly in multiple-disciplinary teams need more information today than people who were working in narrow silos in the past? Absolutely.

Do people at corporate headquarters need *different* information about strategy than people in a business unit? Usually.

Does everyone in a small business need to know everything? Maybe. How do you know for sure? Ask them. If people have performance goals to meet and know they'll benefit when they achieve them, they'll clamor for the information they need to help them win. Given that we're bombarded with information from every nook and cranny of our lives, we're all trying desperately to avoid information overload, which is occurring today far more than even a couple of years ago. People will tell you what they need and what they don't need. But you have to ask.

What about the so-called confidential information that could tip your hand and give a competitor an advantage, or proprietary information about new products? First, you don't want to do anything that will give your competitor an advantage. Second, most of us underestimate what our competition already knows about us. Third, remember relevance—to performance. How can the people in your research and development department create new products and services if they don't have the information they need to create them? They can't. But does that mean everyone needs to know everything the R&D people know? Probably not. Does everybody in the company need to know that you're not sitting on your innovation hands, that you're actively at work to fill your pipeline with new products and services? Yes. Do your sales people need more information about this than, say, your accounting department? Perhaps. Sales people are apt to get pretty frustrated if they don't think someone's working to get new products or services for them to sell.

Some business leaders use the confidentiality banner to cover up for the fact that sharing information requires hard work or that they simply don't trust their people.

I've listened patiently to dozens of business leaders assure me a thousand times over that the reason they don't share "sensitive" strategic information with their people has nothing to do with trust.

"They don't want that kind of information," the regional vice president of a telecommunications company told me. "They just want to do their jobs and go home."

"But," I informed the vice president, "the survey we conducted told us they *do* want more information about company direction and goals."

"They wouldn't understand it anyway," he replied, ignoring my response to his first objection to sharing the information.

I responded again. "These are people who are negotiating mortgages on their homes, planning their retirement, managing college funds for their children, and otherwise trying, probably somewhat successfully, to balance their checkbooks. They wouldn't understand it? Why not?" I asked.

A long pause and then: "I'm afraid of what they would do with the information," he blurted out.

"Do you trust them?" I asked.

"I guess not really!"

Would this year's Super Bowl contestants refuse to share the game plan with their players for fear they would whisper the next play across the line to the opposing team? Of course not. Why? Protecting confidential information increases the chance of winning. When the team wins, it benefits as a team. Its members benefit individually as well. The team members know this. They trust each other to act in the team's best interest because they all have a stake in the action.

Can you treat an organization of 100,000 team members the same as you would an 11-member football team? Of course not. But you can start.

Linkage

Linkage is the stake in the action.

It's the *quid pro quo,* the "what's in it for me." It binds people to the business and to each other.

Linkage can represent "the deal," the contract we make with ourselves. For our contribution to the customer and shareholder, we expect this in return from each other and our organization.

Different people are motivated by different things. Some look for more pay, a promotion, or recognition. Others are motivated by internal drivers, such as personal work ethic, a chance to connect our own sense of worth with a sense of higher purpose, interest in a given task, or the excitement about learning something new.

In interviews with brand managers and sales people at a giant consumer products company to find out what motivated them, they told us that in return for the results they created, they wanted more pay, vacation trips with their families, and membership in the President's Club, a recognition reserved for the best of the best sales people. People in research and development, on the other hand, said that what mattered to them was freedom to present papers at technical symposia, to be left alone at their benches and in their labs to pursue new product ideas, and to have their own business cards.

Very different drivers. Very different motivators.

A seamstress at the Ralph Lauren organization says she comes to work every day "not to sew sleeves on blouses, but to help design a prettier world." She, her work, and the Ralph Lauren brand have connected.

Housekeepers at Ritz-Carlton say they're "proud to be ladies and gentlemen serving ladies and gentlemen." They're not housekeepers, bed makers, or bathroom scrubbers. They go to work each day to deliver an outrageously high level of service to their customers—fellow ladies and gentlemen.

A Gallup organization study of 80,000 managers made it clear that different people have different needs. One-size-fits-all doesn't work. Each employee breathes his or her own "psychological oxygen." "Treat each person as he would like to be treated, bearing in mind who he is," the Gallup study said.

This notion has created a concept some refer to as total rewards. Total rewards goes way beyond rewards as we've traditionally understood them. The total rewards concept creates a large inventory of responses to the various needs people have from their work relationship.

It includes pay and benefits, of course, but also includes flexible work arrangements, learning and development opportunities, an exciting work environment, perks and amenities like concierge services and child care and, of course, stock-purchase, stock-option, and stock award programs.

Many companies, including Starbucks, The Gap, Dupont, and Kimberly Clark, provide stock options to people other than their top leaders. In fact, approximately 6 million nonleader employees received stock options (nonqualified stock options) in 1999.

People need to see a direct connection between the gains they create and the benefits that accrue to them.

One Australian-based contracting company instituted a profit sharing plan for all its employees. When the company did well, the profit sharing plan payout was healthy. When it didn't, it wasn't. That's as it should be. However, frontline employees had no idea how to influence the profit sharing. There was no line of sight between what the employee in the field did and the amount of the profit sharing payout. A profit sharing plan designed to motivate employees wasn't motivating employees fully.

A west coast insurance company created what appeared on paper to be a well-designed incentive plan for which all employees would be eligible. But, the communication of the new incentive plan confused people. Videos had been developed to explain the plan, but the explanations were highly technical. Managers who were supposed to conduct meetings about the new pay plan hadn't been adequately briefed, so they stumbled their way through the discussions and couldn't answer even the most basic questions about job ranges or incentive payouts. The communication process used to explain the new incentive plan wiped out any benefits that the plan may have produced for the company.

When people know what's in it for them, another dot is connected. But knowing that requires knowing what they need to do in order to share in the gain. That's called *role*.

Role

"Hey," a telephone lineman shouted out at an employee meeting, "I've heard this guy Caldwell [the CEO] say we all need to be more market-driven... more market-driven... more market-driven. He's a Johnny One-Note. Now, tell me, how do I climb a damned telephone pole in a more market-driven way?"

We all want to know what we're responsible for, what results we are being held accountable for. You hear it everywhere you turn: Which levers, if any, are exclusively mine to pull and which ones do I share with other team members? What impact do the levers have on the finances of the business, on customer satisfaction, on service, on speed, on whatever is important to the business? When I pull this lever, what happens? When I pull that one, what happens?

"Hey," the telephone lineman was essentially saying, "I'll help you be more market-driven. Just translate what this means to me. What do I need to do differently in my role?"

Years ago, jobs were narrowly defined. "Put this nut on this bolt and then do it again a couple thousand times," people were told. "That's your job." Technology replaced that worker. Today, people in nearly every industry confront more ambiguity around their roles. That's because roles are changing as customers' demands change and as roles become increasingly multifaceted. We're a lot more like a jazz ensemble in our work. The sax carries the melody for a while, then the trumpet kicks in with it and so on around the band. We're a lot less like American football teams, in which each position has an assigned role to play, and a lot more like basketball players, who continually trade off roles, from shooter to blocker to rebounder to defender to assister. True, someone may well be responsible for a specific task, but they're also responsible for contributing to larger goals, such as scoring more points than the other team in order to win the game. In business, someone may well be responsible for a specific task, but they're also responsible for contributing to such larger goals as quality, customer satisfaction, innovation, and cost reduction.

At a utility, total shareholder return may be the ultimate financial goal. But the line crews need to understand that to maximize the financial goal, they need to carefully balance tree-trimming expenses. They can't wait until a tree falls down or customers will be unhappy. But they also can't overtrim the trees, lest they increase costs unnecessarily and influence shareholder return.

In comparison, people in a fast food restaurant need to improve cash flow overall, but they must use their discretionary effort to balance customer cycle time (the elapsed time between when a customer enters the line to order food and the time the order is received), customer satisfaction, and error rates. The restaurant wants customers to have a satisfying experience. They want to serve as many customers as possible. But they don't want to move so fast that they make costly mistakes.

Maximizing business performance is often a balancing act among competing factors and scarce resources. People know this instinctively. But communication about performance often comes across as a dictum to maximize this or that part of the whole, for example, quality, growth, profits, cash flow, expense reduction, or cycle time.

Let's look at Ritz-Carlton again. A housekeeper is expected to freshen the rooms, to be sure. There are a lot of tasks associated with room-freshening. But that person is also responsible for a much larger goal: guest satisfaction. That's why when you pass the housekeeper in the hotel hallway, you get a bright, cheery smile, which is unlike Brand X, whose housekeepers look at their feet when they pass you in the hallway.

If you look lost or confused at a Ritz-Carlton, an employee will quickly step out of her job, whatever it may be, run over to you, and ask if she can help you with anything. She helps you and then springs back to her regular role. Brand X employees act as though they don't notice the lost or confused look on your face. In reality, they probably are just as lost and confused as you are.

Ritz-Carlton connects the dots between their people and their strategy.

"Most of the problems we have in business today are a direct result of our failure to show people how they fit into the big picture," Jack Stack of SRC says. "That failure undermines company after company."

"We put a guy in front of a radial drill and tell him to focus all his attention on drilling a hole as accurately as possible. So he does it. He drills the hole and watches the forging go to the next station, and he sees something fit perfectly into the hole he's just drilled. Then we come back and tell him the company is in trouble because there's something wrong with the way he's using his time. He can't understand. What could be wrong? His job was to drill the hole, and he did it perfectly. So if there's something wrong, it has to be someone else's fault.

"The problem is that we've never trained people to look beyond their machine tools (or their computers, telephones, dollies, trucks, or whatever). So they can't understand how the holes could be perfect and the company could be failing."[19]

For the dots to connect, people need to understand their roles and how they connect to a bigger picture. But they also need the resources to play their roles.

Support

At a town hall meeting in San Antonio, the late Mike Walsh was explaining his six goals for Union Pacific Railroad. The railroad's chairman finished his remarks and invited questions. One worker in the back of the room said, "I hear your goals and I'm all for them. But how can we help you get there if we can't even get the tools we need to run the railroad the way it's supposed to be run? We need help if we're going to help you get where you want to go."

People want to win, but they're often frustrated because they can't get the support they need to deliver. To make matters worse, no one bothers to tell them why the support is unavailable.

Establishing goals and providing the resources needed to achieve the goals sends consistent messages. Establishing goals and not providing those resources sends mixed messages.

Support comes in many forms.

The basic information needed to make decisions, like information about a new product that a chemical company sales rep told me she didn't have but needed before she could do her job.

Tools, like the wire strippers an electrician didn't have but needed, or the two-way radio an electric power company supervisor in the South told me he didn't have but needed to communicate with his team.

Safety equipment, like one railroad employee needed to lift heavy loads without injuring his back.

Technology, like the updated policyholder information a property casualty company employee in California told me she didn't have but needed to respond quickly to a policyholder who phoned with a question.

Training, like the basic-skills training a health care insurance claims processor told me she didn't have but needed to process customer claims accurately ("I just keep sticking it in the machine until it accepts it. I'd be a lot more productive if someone taught me how to run the machine," she told me.)

Promotional support, like the advertising program an automobile brand manager told me he didn't have but needed to promote his cars.

When you communicate that quality, safety, low costs, or speed are important and support people in their endeavors to achieve those things, you're communicating consistent messages. You're saying it; you're doing it, and people will believe you're serious. The dots will connect.

But if you say all those things are important and then don't give people the support they need to achieve them, you're sending mixed messages. You're saying it but you're not doing it. People will doubt your sincerity, and the dots won't connect.

The three communication sources I discussed in Chapter 4 and the five information categories discussed here make up an organization's communication system. When the system is working as an integrated system, performance can reach incredible highs.

Your goal is to manage the communication system as a system.

Part Two: Lessons Learned

- Communication represents all the ways we send, receive, and process information. It's the things we say and don't say. It's the things we do and don't do. You can't not communicate. Communication always bombards the organization.
- Before anyone does anything in our companies, they first *decide* what they're going to do. This is called a decision moment. We need to manage the communication bombardment so that we manage the decision moments people experience before they take action. We want all of their actions to help the company win.
- Connecting people to the business strategy requires connecting the dots to engage people in the business. There are four components of engagement: line of sight, involvement, information sharing, and rewards and recognition.
- Companies that connect the dots value their people. They manage communication as a core business process. The CEO is the communication champion.
- Three communication sources influence what we do: leadership, the systems infrastructure, and formal communication channels. Leadership and the systems infrastructure have the most influence, but all three are important.
- People will become engaged in helping the business win when they understand:
  - Context—the big picture.
  - Vision and strategy—what the business needs to become and how it plans to do it.

- Linkage—what's in it for me.
- Role—expectations of me and our team.
- Support—the resources people have to help create success.

PART THREE

The Communication System

CHAPTER 8

Say and Do— A Sailing Metaphor

There's nothing more agonizing than a boat and a crew without a system—an order of events, a team plan, and clear communication.[20]

— Bill Allen

Managing communication to connect the dots is a lot like working with a sailboat. Sailing requires a strong grounding in some essential principles in order to steer effectively through the decision moments that make for success or failure.

When sailing, the skipper must negotiate external forces beyond his control, namely water and wind. When managing communication, the business leader must negotiate external forces beyond her control, namely competitors, customers, material shortages, foreign currencies, and government regulation.

When sailing, the skipper needs to maintain continuous focus or he could lose boat speed, stray off course, damage the boat, or hurt or lose a crew member. When managing communication, the business leader needs to maintain continuous focus or the organization could lose momentum, stray off course, and hurt or lose its people.

Over the years, good skippers learn to trust their intuition, their instincts. They learn that there are times when action is called for, not always because there's a mountain of data to back it up, but sometimes because it just feels right. There's a voice deep inside the brain that says, "It's time to change course" or "You probably ought to tweak that mainsail a tad." Over the years, business leaders learn that analytical rigor has value, but that it shouldn't replace common sense or a good hunch. Certain decisions just feel right. Sometimes intuition tells us, "We've got to act now!"

Winning sailboat races demands continuous crew interaction regarding goals, strategies and tactics for winning, roles, and how to celebrate a victory. Winning in business demands continuous teammate interaction. The dialogues are similar.

Sailing requires managing a relatively complex system, all the stuff that's under the boat—like the rudder, hull, and keel—and all the stuff that's out of the water, such as most of the boat, the lines, and the sails—especially the sails. Sails have to be adjusted—or trimmed—as a system to propel the boat forward efficiently. Multiple sails on a sailboat must work together to achieve maximum efficiency. But the sails also need to work in harmony with what's under the boat.

When the wind shifts, the entire sailing system needs to be adjusted. Sometimes, the adjustment is a minor tweak. Other times, it requires a change in heading, or significant sail adjustment. In either case, the boat needs to be managed as an integrated system rather than as a collection of parts. The adjustments need to happen quickly. A good skipper won't let a sail remain unadjusted or out of trim for even a few seconds. Sailboat races are sometimes won by seconds.

Back to the realm of business, an organization's communication system has two primary components: sources and content. We discussed both at length in Chapters 4 through 7. The three communication sources are like the sails on a sailboat (Figure 8-1). Imagine a two-masted sailboat. In the figure, the largest sail, the foresail, represents leadership, because in normal conditions employees tell us that leadership is the biggest driver of what they'd do just as on a sailboat the foresail is usually the biggest sail. The mainsail represents the system's infrastructure. Employees tell us that it's the second largest driver. The third sail, the mizzen, represents the formal communication media. It's the smallest, just as the formal communication media acting alone usually have the smallest impact on performance.

To reach the highest level of performance, communication must be managed as a system. Sources and content must work in harmony. When business conditions change because of new technology or changing customer demands, the system needs to be adjusted. As in sailing, sometimes it's a minor tweak here and there. But other times might require a major alteration. For instance, the winds of technology have re-

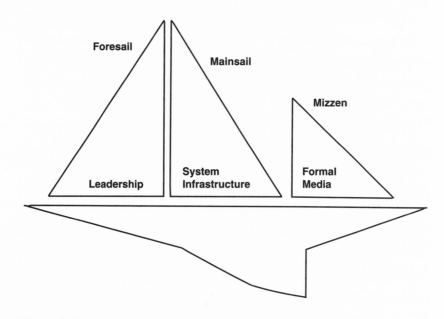

Figure 8-1.

quired a major change in the way we manage information through intranets. The winds of changing work-force values have required major shifts in the way we involve people and in how we define rewards.

In a competitive environment, a business leader can't afford to have a misaligned communication system any more than a racing yachtsman can win with misaligned sails.

When the communication system is aligned, people inside the business will make the right decisions when they encounter decision moments. They'll take the actions that are needed to improve organizational and financial performance. When misaligned, people become confused. Decision moments are managed helter-skelter. Actions push the organization in multiple directions. The result: lower productivity, higher costs, reduced quality and service, a sluggish business that's vulnerable.

Businesses are more vulnerable to communication system misalignment during periods of significant change—a restructuring, downsizing, merger, or acquisition. During these kinds of earthshaking events (see Chapter 15), business leaders are tempted to reach for the sail that's easiest to trim, that little mizzen, i.e., the formal communication media. It's more than the easy way out; it's also a major mistake. First, the formal communication media and channels have little influence on the organization. The sail maker didn't intend for that little sail to do the heavy work. Second, unless all the three sources— and the content—are managed together as a system during an earthshaking event, adjusting the formal communication media alone is likely to throw the *say* communication and *do* communication out of whack. And because addressing the formal media comes at a cost, it's a cost that's rarely recouped in terms of performance.

Not long ago, I received a call on a Saturday afternoon from the vice president of human resources of a large shipping company. He told me the company would announce on the following Thursday that they were being acquired by another shipping company. "We'd like to talk to you about communicating this to our employees," he said. When I met with company leadership the following Tuesday (two days before the scheduled announcement), it became clear that their idea of "communicating this to our employees" involved no more than a one-page memo, which, at the meeting's outset, they presented for my review. That was it. One two-page memo was supposed to address all the anxieties, fears, questions, and concerns about what the acquisition was all about and what it meant to the people in the company.

How have we become so callused?

When a skipper throws the sails out of alignment or when a business leader throws the communication system out of alignment by managing only one source, the crew reaction is similar. People become confused. They sense a lack of direction. They get frustrated. They wonder: "Hey, what's going on here? Is anybody at the helm?"

Unless the leader aligns the sails or the communication system, both races can be lost.

When there's a business performance problem, there's almost always a flaw in the communication system. The leader's goal is to find the flaw and remove it. *(See Chapter 11 for more on this.)*

Communication bombards us continuously. You can't turn it off, no more than you can turn off the wind. There's a sailing aphorism that goes: "You can't adjust the wind, but you can always adjust the sails." I'm often amused when business leaders make a decision about a particular issue and then ask each other: "Should we communicate this to the troops?" as though they have a choice. They *don't* have a choice. Whatever decision was made *will* be communicated—probably first in a chat room or lunchroom—whether the leadership likes it or not. The more appropriate question is, "Should we *manage* the communication or let it manage itself?" It's the equivalent of asking: "Shall we just let the sails luff (flap around), or should we trim them to manage the boat better?" When there's wind, the sails will continue to move the boat somewhere, but it may be in circles or until the sailboat just drifts. Similarly, the communication system will continue to bombard the organization whether we want it to or not. People will act based on what they hear, see, and read. If the objective is to engage people and raise performance, we have only one choice: to manage the system. Failure to do so may cause the business to go in circles or drift. It also is tantamount to leadership abdication.

Leaders who want to connect the dots and create maximum performance will always choose to manage the communication system rather than let it manage itself.

This kind of systems thinking relative to communication management reflects what actually occurs in organizations. But put in this new and more realistic light, business leaders are inclined to ask: "Who can I turn to for advice in this area? Who in my company is equipped to partner with me to improve the way we manage communication and performance?"

Viewed systemically, communication isn't a narrow functional discipline. Instead, it draws upon a variety of disciplines, including information technology, human resources, organizational development and training, finance, and the more traditional communication function, as well as—and especially—line management. To respond to this more accurate view of communication management, communication functions are attempting to reinvent themselves to be in a better position to partner with leaders and other line managers. You'll learn more about this in Part Six. But no amount of reinvention will preclude addressing communication management from a broader-based, multidisciplinary perspective.

Because that's the way organizations function in real time.

CHAPTER 9

Tell Me the Story

Tell them the truth, first, because it's the right thing to do, and second, they'll find out anyway.

— Paul Galvin, founder, Motorola

W hat's the story, Tom? Tell me the story, Tom. I want to know the story."

Tom Downs stood in his office doorway at Amtrak headquarters in Washington, D.C. He'd been the railroad's chairman and CEO for only a few weeks. His first few weeks had been devoted to listening, primarily to Amtrak employees and customers. He'd just returned from a series of meetings with railroad employees along the Northeast Corridor, that stretch of track from Washington to Boston.

"Our people want to know the story," Downs told me. "They want to know what's going on. They want to know the same things that you and I want to know about our jobs. They don't want anything mysterious—just the straight stuff, the truth."

"So," he continued, "we need to be able to tell our story, an honest, credible story that our management team can communicate throughout the corporation. It's something we've got to talk and walk," Downs said.

Over the next couple of weeks, Downs created what he referred to as "The Amtrak Story," literally a story about Amtrak's past, present, and future.

He assembled his top 115 managers at a conference center west of Washington. Although many of these managers had been at Amtrak since it was created in 1971, Downs was the first CEO to bring the top management together in one room.

Few at the conference had met Downs. He was an outsider. He didn't come up through the ranks as many Amtrak managers had. Most of the managers had come to the conference to take the measure of their new CEO.

Roughly 30 seconds after Downs had been introduced, he told his managers, "If you go away remembering absolutely nothing else about this meeting, I want you to remember one thing: Always tell the truth. Tell the truth to each other, to our employees, to our customers, to our communities, and to the political and regulatory bodies that we associate with. Always tell the truth."

Always tell the truth!

Why is this remarkable? I've worked with and been around a handful of American railroads. I've conducted culture assessments at two very different railroads, one, a passenger railroad, the other, a freight railroad. I've spoken with managers of railroads with whom I've had little association. I've addressed several railroad associations. I'm convinced that in the United States, a railroad culture is a railroad culture.

In short, a railroad culture represents the last bastion of organizational militarism. Railroads are autocratic, run by older white males, and thick with middle managers who spend their days shouting orders because their bosses are shouting orders at them. No one asks anyone else for their ideas for fear it would represent a sign of weakness. Management is management and labor is labor. Neither trusts the other.

So here's Downs in front of 115 Amtrak managers for the first time and he's asking them to do one simple little thing—*always tell the truth*. If every one of these 115 managers did as Downs asked, they could, as a group, do severe damage to the traditional railroad culture. That would be good.

Of course, Downs knew this. How simple: no long-winded values statement, just a single four-word sentence could turn the railroad culture on its ear and begin the long process of needed improvement.

Then he told the story Amtrak employees had begged him to tell. It was the story he wanted to tell.

Here's how it went.

> This is the story of a railroad that must become obsessed with serving its customers or it will go the way of drive-in theaters, full-service gas stations, and downtown shopping.

Change or die! He hits them hard in the first sentence. Then he continues the story, providing these leaders with information in each of the five information categories.

> Amtrak was born old. It opened for business in 1971 with 450 worn-out locomotives, 40-year-old, steam-heated passenger cars, an antiquated reservation system, and several inefficient maintenance facilities owned by other railroads.
>
> There have been many improvements over the years. But the railroad never caught up.

Notice how he builds the context of the message, the framework for the rest of the story.

> Since its birth, Amtrak's nearly 25,000 hardworking, railroad-loving employees fought and cursed old systems, processes, and equipment in order to do their jobs. It's a wonder they did as well as they did.

Downs is careful not to criticize Amtrak people or what they have done. Amtrak's problems weren't people problems. He acknowledged that what people had done was the best they could do, that it was right for the time.

But that was then. This is now.

A transition from the past to the future.

Today the railroad is in trouble, big, deep trouble.

This is what some refer to as the burning platform.

Equipment is still old and in disrepair. In an effort to live within our budgets, we've repaired old equipment at the expense of buying new equipment.

We've had bad luck. Weather and accidents caused by factors out of our control have been expensive and placed a cloud over the railroad.

Customer expectations are accelerating as airlines work hard to meet customer needs for high quality, service, and value.

A constant struggle to reduce costs has reduced service.

An antiquated organizational structure and inadequate resources continue to make it difficult for our 25,000 employees to serve their customers. People can endure only so much before they lose the spirit and enthusiasm that's necessary to win in today's environment.

Customers feel it. They're looking to other forms of transportation, many who've undergone the kinds of changes we must undergo.

Already this year, we're $109 million behind our original forecast. This is the equivalent of 54 new low-level cars, 36 locomotives, salaries for 2400 customer service employees for a year, or huge improvements in our Sunnyside, Beach Grove, or Wilmington facilities.

He's building the burning platform in a way people can relate to, hard realities they can understand and work with.

We're in a deep hole. We're in deep trouble.

A return to the burning platform, then on to what Amtrak needs to build.

For Amtrak to survive, we must fundamentally change the organization.

Fundamental does not mean tweak here, fine tune there. It does not mean do what we've always done, but better.

He's painting a picture of what change and improvement mean and don't mean. He then describes the vision and strategy.

Amtrak must be reinvented. It must be reinvented in the form of a modern, customer-obsessed, high-performing organization.

It must begin with an intense and simultaneous focus on the two most important groups of people in Amtrak's world—our customers and our employees.

Downs knew that Amtrak people were obsessive about serving customers. But he realized that they were frustrated by their inability to get the systems to work for them. They were old, tired, and designed to serve the bosses, not the customer.

We must create a partnership between our customers, who demand quality, service, and value, and our employees, who get up every day wanting to do what's right by the customer.

This kind of partnership will create a financially strong

business. A financially strong business will be very attractive to our other business partners at the federal, state, and local levels.

We have already begun to reinvent Amtrak. Here's what we're doing:

He lists a dozen or so initiatives that are underway. His point: We all have a responsibility to fix the railroad. He is describing how he is leading the way.

What does reinventing Amtrak mean?

For leaders throughout Amtrak it means communicating with everything they say and do that we have no choice but to create a fundamentally different railroad—a railroad that is dramatically tilted toward the customer. Amtrak leaders must be in charge of dramatically improving the system, removing system defects that cause dissatisfied customers. Our leaders must look for every opportunity to make sure that our employees have the resources—including money, tools, and information—needed to take care of the customers.

For all our employees, it means viewing the customer as your only boss. Our employees have a responsibility to identify areas for improvement and then help improve them. They need to seek the skills, information, and tools they need to improve quality, service, and value.

Reinventing Amtrak will mean assuming different roles and responsibilities. It will mean trying new things on behalf of the customer.

He then segues into the information category called *linkage*— what's in it for me. Note his appeal to a sense of pride and purpose.

Reinventing Amtrak also means a new relationship between the organization and our employees. Amtrak was born out of a paternalistic and authoritarian environment. The company knew what was best for its employees. If the employees did as they were told, the organization would take care of them—provide regular pay increases and some measure of job security. The paternalistic relationship may have worked well in the past. It doesn't today. World-class performance around quality, service, costs, speed, and innovation doesn't come from controlled, protected people who are taken care of. It comes from informed, engaged business people who are held accountable for the organization's success. That's the Amtrak we must create.

Many people will find the process of reinventing Amtrak to be an exciting and rewarding one. Some will be uncomfortable in the new environment. They may find comfort going elsewhere. We thank them for their contributions and recognize them as important Amtrak alumni.

He's saying it's okay to say no to the new way. In effect, he's saying: "I realize this new way isn't what you signed up for. You have the opportunity to opt out. It's okay to opt out." But opting out means you're not at Amtrak.

We are America's railroad. We cannot continue to survive if we don't reinvent Amtrak. We can become the world's best passenger railroad.

It will take time, down-in-the-trenches hard work, and an unwavering focus on our customers and our employees. Getting there will be at once exciting and painful, exhilarating and frustrating. But when we get there, it will have been worth the ride.

When he finished, Amtrak's managers gave him a standing ovation. He'd said things they all knew and felt, but that nobody had said until Downs said them.

"Tell the story again and again," Downs importuned his managers. "And just when you think you've told it enough times, tell it one more time."

Throughout the Tom Downs years at Amtrak, there were two communication principles at work at Amtrak: (1) *Always tell the story*, and (2) *Always tell the truth.*

The story Downs told was the story he wanted every Amtrak employee to experience, not just hear and read. He wanted to connect people and what they did to a greater purpose, a strategy, a vision.

I call this kind of story a focused message. It's a credible story, what we tell one another to explain something deep yet simple about the world in which we live and work. A story gains credibility when it connects immediately with what we believe and takes us to a deeper understanding of what we must do.

A focused message is a set of intricately woven details—each a message in itself—that everyone in the business needs to understand in order for the business to win.

The focused message should incorporate all five information categories: context, vision and strategy, linkage, role, and support. Leave out a category and the dots probably won't connect.

Certainly, the focused message must be communicated with words. But crafting the words represents the easy part. Anyone can put words on paper, just as anyone can create a plan for winning a game. Execution leads to success or failure. I've seen many business leaders spend hours upon hours arguing over insignificant wording differences, commas, and capitalization when they try to craft messages to their people, yet fail to spend the time that's truly needed on what the words really mean to the core of the enterprise. They talk in lofty words and phrases but forget that real people trying to decipher what those lofty phrases mean are, in real life, the people who talk to customers, who purchase raw materials, who make corporate investments, who spend company money, and who create the new products that win in the marketplace.

Accountability for what? Protecting the old order? Protecting the customer? Results? Following procedures? How will people be held accountable?

Recognize and reward achievement? What kind of achievement? Follow-the-rules kind of achievement? A lot of effort? Results? What kind of results?

You get the picture.

Leaders must be specific. They have to paint a clear picture of what the focused message means to the people in their organizations. With the focused message clearly in mind, people are more apt to make the right decisions when they encounter decision moments.

Operationalizing the focused message is the first step toward managing the communication system consistently so that the *say* communication and *do* communication send consistent messages. Failing to identify the implications of the focused message to the rest of the operation is apt to result in spewing out mixed messages and damaging your credibility as a leader.

Tom Downs was a new leader. He needed to change the organization. He knew organizations don't change unless people do. He knew he couldn't do it without the active participation and engagement of those who would make the changes.

He knew that doing so meant that he had to have a credible, plausible story that everyone in the organization could understand. He knew he needed help in telling the story. He knew the story needed to be told through what was said and what was done.

Downs knew that leaders need to say it *and* do it to link people to strategy, to connect the dots.

CHAPTER 10

Stories Start with Leaders

Being a leader is a hard job—maybe the hardest job there is. But once you've chosen it, you have a moral obligation to be your best self.

— Paul Wieand, founder of Emotional
Intelligence and former CEO of
Independence Bancorp[21]

The story represents the brush strokes that flow from dot to dot. The leader's job is to guide the brush. No one can do it.

Connecting the dots begins smack dab at the hierarchic top with the CEO, the hospital administrator, the office leader, the school superintendent, the cabinet secretary, the store owner, whoever sits in that pivotal number-one leadership role.

If the ultimate leader doesn't champion the effort, it won't be perceived as important. If it's not perceived as important, it's not likely to get done.

How it gets done depends on a lot of factors, including size of the business, industry position, your culture, competitive threats, leadership styles and personalities, relations with labor unions, financial position and *what you're willing to do.*

As the leader, you need to conduct a realistic self-examination. What can you focus on and for how long? What are you willing to make work? What's of lesser importance to you. What are the tradeoffs associated with taking certain actions, such as holding your own team accountable? For instance, might you lose a good manager who always delivers the numbers if you insist that his performance bonus requires delivering the numbers *and* building an engaged team? How much time do you have? Are you hemorrhaging? Or is one business unit's performance out of sync with the others? (Take a look at Chapter 17 and its questionnaire. It has helped many business leaders conduct a self-examination to determine what they are and aren't willing to do.)

Not too many years ago, it was the fashion to launch what was referred to as large scale culture change; some called it transformational change. It tended to work for smaller organizations. But transformational change requires transformational leadership. Transformational leaders are in short supply, and even for them transformational change is difficult. Most leaders who begin connecting the dots start with a piece of the business, an issue or a specific flaw in the communication system.

I worked with a business leader in a publishing operation who wanted to begin by building business literacy. He wanted the people in his company to have a better understanding of the marketplace and how it was affecting the company. He wanted people to know how the company made money, how it "worked." When he began, he understood that when he addressed only a piece of the engagement puzzle, the gains he'd make would be limited. But, he wanted to start there and then slowly move through the other engagement components.

Another industrial company's CEO emphasized economic value added (EVA). He started by improving line of sight, making sure everyone in the company understood how they could influence growth and costs.

A utility leader on the west coast focused on the reward system because an employee survey reported that people didn't think there was anything "in it for them" when they contributed to company results.

Another utility leader stayed away from the reward system because rewards were negotiated with his labor union. He worked to improve line of sight, involvement, and information sharing.

Some leaders attack geographic areas or business units. An insurance company created four pilot sites within its branch offices and made huge improvements before expanding the pilots to five more branches.

Focusing efforts makes sense. However, it's important to know that when you focus on only one engagement component, for instance, you will not realize the gains that you might otherwise generate if you focus on making sure all four engagement components are strong. The total quality movement of a few years ago offers us some lessons. Hundreds of companies sent thousands of employees off to quality training. In classrooms, people learned the definition of quality and were taught problem-solving techniques, pareto charts, cause-and-effect diagrams, run flow charts and all the rest. Then they went back to their workplaces and *nothing happened.*

Why? Because nothing really changed. The training was interesting. But, back at the workplace, the manager or supervisor was the same manager or supervisor as before. The environment was the same. The systems were the same. Nothing changed. As a result, customer satisfaction didn't improve. Total quality, to these companies, was a program, not a mindset or way of life.

The same is true with engagement. Many companies have invested a lot of money on business literacy. They've spent money on learning

151

maps, computer simulated games and value trees, all potentially wonderful tools to help deliver business literacy. But, unless the educational effort is reinforced and sustained back at the work site, not much good usually comes of the business literacy investment.

Successful Pilot or Test Site Criteria

Pilots or test sites often can help get the momentum going for a larger effort. Here are five conditions that contribute to a successful pilot or test site:

1. The site is headed by an assertive, progressive leader who values people and whose people respect him or her.
2. The site is relatively self-contained. You can identify site-specific performance measures that need to be improved and that people within the site can directly influence.
3. Current performance is low, which makes it easier to generate improvements (compared to a location where performance is already high).
4. The number of people at the site is relatively small—less than 1000; ideally 300 to 400.
5. The site can be relatively exempt from certain corporate policies or systems (e.g., restrictive pay plans).

Even starting small can represent hard work at first. I've had initial meetings with many business leaders who said they had to improve communication, had to get their people more on board. Some have had a specific goal: to make *Fortune's* list of "Best Companies to Work for in America." "I want to make the list," the CEO of a west coast financial organization told my colleagues and me. "Show me what I need to do to make the list." We did and he gave up before he got started.

Others have been more realistic. They dived in and stayed with it. Some made modest gains; others huge gains.

Open-book pioneer Jack Stack only half jokingly points out that once he got everyone on board thinking and acting like business owners, he wasn't the only one in the company with the nightmares. Everyone in the company was worrying about what he was worrying about.

vividly and powerfully that it also becomes their vision. An A leader has enormous personal energy... and the ability to energize others. An A leader has 'edge,' the instinct and courage to make the tough calls. As we go forward, there will be nothing but A's in every leadership position in the company. They will be the best in the world and they will act to field teams consisting of nothing but A players."

Leadership development

GE's Management Institute in Crotonville, New York, is among the world's best leadership academies. Many companies have patterned their leadership institutes or universities after GE's Crotonville, as the management institute is referred to. Jack Welch doesn't leave the training to the trainers, although they are some of the world's best. Welch serves as faculty, as do other members of his top team. I've been in the pit* when Welch met with one of my client's leadership teams. He is a powerful teacher. An hour with Welch in that room leaves no doubt why he has developed one of the best corporate leadership's teams in the world.

At Toyota's huge Georgetown, Kentucky, manufacturing plant, Masamoto Amezawa, president of the operation, says: "It's my job to teach my managers. Others can play a role. But teaching is an important job for me."

FedEx is nearly fanatical about its Managerial Communication Climate and Competence process, which ties leadership development to its assessment process. Ed Robertson, the company's manager of employee communication and one of the process developers explains: "Our communication philosophy is grounded in the Federal Express corporate People-Service-Profit philosophy, which is: Take care of our people and they, in turn, will deliver the impeccable service de-

---

*There's a large training room at the GE Management Institute. It's set up as a theater, with theater seats rising toward the back of the room. The room's "stage" is often referred to as the pit.

manded by our customers, who will reward us with the profitability necessary to secure our future.

"The company places tremendous importance on the value of its employees as the primary reason for success. Communication then becomes the primary link with all employees to organize their individual mental and physical energies into a unified force for achieving corporate excellence." Robertson says the development process is targeted at "developing managers as competent communicators by providing communication skill-building opportunities, installing communication policies and practices, and continually reinforcing the importance of communication as a key factor in effective leadership."

Leadership accountability

These companies hold leaders accountable for results—financial results and people results. Accountability means consequences. There are good consequences for being a good leader. Poor leaders are given attention, support, and coaching. If poor leaders continue to be poor leaders, they're offered other opportunities, or they go elsewhere where they may feel more comfortable.

Good leadership development is wasted if the people receiving the development aren't held accountable for what they've learned.

"I know what it says on paper," says a top manager at a chemical company. "But all of us around here know what it *really* takes to get ahead. Make your numbers and they'll turn their backs on all the people stuff."

Some form of multi-source or 360-degree feedback is usually used to assess leaders' performance. A multi-source assessment or 360-degree feedback represents an assessment by a leader's leader, peers, and the employees he or she's leading.

Top managers at UnumProvident are assessed using a 40-question survey each year. Employees and peers evaluate leaders on how well they "visualize and clearly paint an exciting vision" and how well they "inspire others to that vision."

FedEx's Fred Smith expects employees to evaluate everyone in a leadership position on a 29-item questionnaire. It's part of the company's Survey-Feedback-Action Process, or SFA. The questionnaire is replete with questions associated with communication, listening, involvement, and treating people with dignity and respect.

The assessments are then used to help determine compensation adjustments, incentive pay-outs and additional developmental needs.

Goal Clarity

At a high-tech company in California one morning, a 23-year-old programmer picked up the current edition of the employee publication and read a cover story quoting the company's president. In the article the president discussed his goals for the company. There were financial goals revolving around "being more profitable" and "growing the company quickly." The CEO also spoke about becoming a learning organization. The article carried no details about any of the three goals mentioned, no discussion of how much growth or how much profit, no definition of what a learning organization was or looked like,* no discussion of priorities or measures, no references to how to find out more.

The programmer took the article to her manager and asked if he knew any more about the president's goals than what the article stated. He told her this was the first he'd heard of the goals. She knew as

*In 1990 MIT professor Peter Senge published *The Fifth Discipline: The Art and Practice of the Learning Organization.* It offered a vision of workplaces that were humane and of companies that were created around learning. He's since published two sequels to the book.

much as he did, he told her. She asked if the goals meant anything for her or her job. The manager said he didn't think so. "He talks about his goals once a year," the manager explained about the president. "His goals are just pie-in-the-sky stuff. They never really mean anything to the people who do the work."

This vignette happens daily in businesses. Leaders announce lofty goals without explaining what they mean to the people who have to implement them. It's similar to telling the crew on a sailboat that I have a destination in mind, I am not going to tell them what it is, yet I want them to help get us there. It *is* as crazy as it sounds.

As you can see from Figure 10-1, there's a considerable distance between the lofty goals and the person who has to achieve them. The dots don't connect.

Figure 10-1.

Leadership's role is to reach agreement on goals and performance targets—with appropriate input from those who will be held accountable for hitting the targets—and then to carefully explain them to the people in the organization who have to deliver. What are we trying to accomplish? What numbers are important and why? Open-book companies talk about critical numbers.

"The critical number is the number that can take out an organization," says Jack Stack. "Critical numbers are the numbers that drive a business's key objectives," says John Case in *The Open Book Experience.* "They're the numbers that must move in the right direction if the business is to succeed in what it's trying to do *right now.*

Scott McNealy, CEO of Sun Microsystems, focuses everyone on system uptime which is how often Sun systems are up and running at the company's customer locations.

Barbara Cassani, CEO of London-based Go Fly Ltd., a start-up, low-fare airline, needs to be cost-focused. She monitors cost per available seat kilometer, which collapses all costs into a single number.

Numbers need to be explained in ways that can be understood by the people who have to deliver. (Figure 10-2 shows how people need to understand the link between corporate, business unit, team and personal goals and actions.) In this figure, the dots connect.

Your company may have a 5 percent return-on-sales (ROS) goal, but that means little to the person on the line whose job it is to package the product for shipment unless the ROS goal's meaning has been explained. Most employees I interview have not passed a course in mind reading. What does it mean to her individually? What's her role? What does she need to do more of or less of for the company to make its ROS target? To the filler operator in a brewery, earnings before interest and taxes (EBIT) simply means keep quality high, manage waste and costs. "I know there are specific things within my control that can help EBIT," the filler operator told me. "So, I manage those

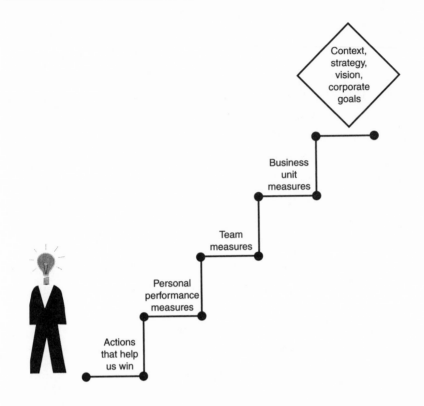

Figure 10-2.

things as well as I can. If we all manage what's within our control, we'll beat the competition," she said.

Nonfinancial numbers need to connect to financial measures. 3M's vision is to be the most innovative enterprise and the preferred supplier. In a document sent to shareholders and employees, it said it's long-term financial goals were 10 percent-plus earnings-per-share growth, 25 percent-plus return on capital employed, and a 20 to 25 percent return on equity. Its innovation goal, which is a direct contributor to those financial goals, was to have 30 percent of sales from products newly introduced over the last four years. Those goals are explained clearly to people in each business unit so they understand their contribution to the corporate goals and what they have to do to help the larger team win. When 3M does this, they're helping to connect their people and what they do to the business strategy.

Contrast 3M's approach with the approach taken by the leadership of a certain construction materials company. In broad strokes, it told employees that the company's goals were to raise return on sales, improve employee retention, increase the number of teams at work, reduce the number of days worked without an accident, improve employee satisfaction scores, and increase the number of hours people were in training. This hodge-podge of seemingly unrelated goals only confused people. The goals lacked focus and integration. And in fact, the company could hit most of those goals and still go out of business.

Communication Policy or Guidelines

Two large companies merged. The acquiring company was relatively tight-lipped. Its communication philosophy was conservative. The acquired company had always shared a lot of information among its people. The two philosophies clashed during the merger. The acquirer remained close to the vest with information. The open company wanted to share information it had traditionally shared with its people. "Everything, every sentence, is debated, edited, and debated again," the head of communication remarked. "Then the two companies have to come together and discuss if we're going to say anything and if we are what it's going to be. You know who wins? The lawyers. We go through this with everything. It's a communications nightmare."

Many business leaders appear afraid to say, "We don't know yet. We don't have the answers yet." We all know that our leaders can't and don't have all the answers. Admitting "I don't know" can help make leaders authentic.

In a situation such as the one where the tight-lipped company acquired the open company, people in the open company experience the most frustration. People in the closed company haven't lost anything they've come to expect. But in a more open company, people are used to a leadership that values people and encourages information sharing as a way to boost performance. People who lose information they've always had feel as though a valuable tool has been taken away from them, information they've counted on to help them perform is being withheld. They've become dependent on information to succeed. "It feels as though someone just came up and tied my arm behind me," one employee in the acquiring company told me. And they wonder, of course, what kind of leadership they've inherited, if any.

Some businesses are open; some remain very secretive. Tight-lipped companies fall toward the left-hand side of the communication continuum shown in Figure 10-3, open companies toward the right.

Few companies reside on the poles. Most fall somewhere between "need to know" and "full disclosure." As a business leader, you need to decide what you and your team will share and what you won't share. You need to base your decisions on what people need—from their perspective, not just yours—in order to perform at increasingly higher levels. Remember, connecting the dots isn't something you do because

Figure 10-3. The communication continuum.

it's nice. Leaders connect the dots because in a highly competitive business world, informed people outperform uninformed people, all else being equal. So where are you on the continuum? Where should you be? Where will you derive the performance gains? Although full disclosure shouldn't necessarily be every leader's goal, "need to know" shouldn't be either. Most companies will generate correspondingly higher performance as they move right on the continuum.

Moreover, you need to decide this as a team so you can take the guesswork out of communication management. There's enough ambiguity to manage in business these days without needlessly adding to it.

Don't be surprised if your discussions on communication issues take you to deeper philosophical levels regarding your beliefs in people and their value. Your communication philosophy in many respects reflects your philosophy about people, how much you trust them, and how much you should protect them or permit them to make choices.

As you create your policy or guidelines, make sure you and your leadership team are absolutely clear about what you mean. "Open communication" can mean different things to different people.

As an example, I was working with a telecommunications company's CEO and his leadership team. The team wanted to "open up the organization," as they put it, in an effort to generate higher commitment levels from their people.

I asked the group what they meant by "open."

"You know, everything, no secrets, open," Jerry, the CEO, said. The group silently nodded in agreement.

"So," I replied, "you'll share everyone's pay information with everyone else."

"Well, no, I don't think we'd do that," Jerry said.

"Okay, so pay information is all that you won't share?" I asked.

"I would say so," Jerry replied.

I pointed to Lou, his chief financial officer, and asked Jerry: "If you caught Lou with his hand in the till and you fired him as a result of it, would you communicate the details to everyone in the organization?"

Jerry: "Absolutely not! I would want to preserve his dignity."

I continued to ask them whether they'd share information about a variety of sensitive subjects. With each one I offered, I gave them what I believed to be the pros and cons of sharing. In the end, they agreed on being completely open on about half of the subjects. At the end of the exercise, Jerry looked at me and laughed: "Okay, Jim, I guess we really want to be a 'sort-of-open company'."

Jerry and his team had rejected sharing information on some issues, to be sure. But, more importantly, they'd agreed to aspire to a higher level of openness than had existed in their organization. They reached the decision together. They were prepared to put together a plan to achieve their aspiration.

Had the team not gone through this simple process, they'd probably nodded their heads in agreement when Jerry announced that he wanted to "open up the organization." That would have been that. Except that after the meeting, Ellen, the head of marketing, would manage according to her definition of openness, which was the equivalent of open-book management where her people would work from the cash flow statement, income statement, and balance sheet. On the other hand, Bob, who headed the regulatory department, would manage according to his definition of openness, which was something akin to the old television show, "I've Got a Secret." When people from each of their groups needed to work together, the combined team would be operating from vastly different knowledge bases.

A notable brewing company's leadership team came to a broad-scale agreement on the definition of open communication they wanted among employees. They agreed both on what it meant and what it didn't mean. Sometimes it's not until the leadership team understands the difference between what it does and doesn't mean, that it really understands what it *does* mean.

Open communication may mean this...	But not this...
Share financial statements for a brewery.	Share with all employees the cash flow, income statement, and balance sheet for the company.
Explain customer satisfaction drivers.	Explain customer satisfaction data for each customer to all employees.
Everyone understands what it takes to share in the gain-sharing program.	Everyone knows everyone else's annual compensation.
It is explained to plant employees how our product is made.	The exact formulation of specific brands is explained to employees.
Everyone knows innovation is important to our future success.	Proprietary R&D information is shared with every employee.

Create a Focused Message or Story

In Chapter 9, I talked about the focused message and the story that Tom Downs created when he took Amtrak's helm. Many other CEOs have created focused messages, some brief, to-the-point "bullets," some more elaborate statements. One region of GTE created a four-bullet story, backed up by a comprehensive implementation plan. Earnie Deavenport, chairman and CEO at Eastman Chemical, personally led the effort to create *The Eastman Story,* a detailed focused message that stipulates what each element of the story means to people throughout the company.

Chapter 9 describes how the focused message acts as a communication filter. Just as in cooking you use a filter or strainer to keep the wrong ingredients from getting into a soup, a focused message, used properly, helps keep the wrong information from getting into the organization. The focused message should include the five information categories:

- Context
- Vision/strategy

- Linkage
- Role
- Support

Once you've created a focused message, you can then test everything you say and do against it. In other words, everything you say and do should help communicate the focused message. If something doesn't, either don't say it or don't do it or change the focused message.

The focused message acts as a framework for other substories that can be developed and deployed by other leaders as they work to support the corporate goal in their specific areas of responsibility.

A focused message *is not* a set of messages exclusively for top-down delivery. That is, it's not something you necessarily "roll out" to your people. It's a working document that serves as your communication guide. Of course, you can communicate the focused message to your people as Tom Downs did. But if you communicate it through what you say, you must also be prepared to deliver on it through what you do. For instance, if the strategy portion of your focused message states: "To grow profitably by focusing resources on businesses offering the best growth potential and managing the remaining businesses to grow revenues for investment," you need to *do* what it says you'll do, and when you do make it clear to your people that you are delivering on your strategy message.

If the linkage section of your story states something like: "Because our performance, stock price, and other incentives are tied to our financial performance as a company, we'll all gain economically when the company succeeds economically," you need to make sure that there's a direct correlation between what people do and their financial rewards, that they *understand* that correlation, and that they know how to act on it.

As you can see from these two examples, the story isn't just a pile of words. It consists of words, but it's the supporting actions that render it useful. Say it; do it!

Years of helping leadership teams craft their stories have taught me that the words are the easiest part. Listing the actions to be taken alongside the words is where the debate runs strongest.

I recommend that for each information category, you have two columns, one for the say communication, one for the *do*. It might look like this:

Information Category	When we say this...	It means we must do this...
Context	Your message about the big picture	Actions you will take to communicate about the external environment (e.g., customers, competitors, regulatory pressures, business cycles).
Vision/Strategy	Your message about what you want to be and how you plan to get there.	Actions you will take to realize the vision and implement the strategy (e.g., improve quality or service, increase speed-to-market, seek acquisitions, simplify work processes, focus on specific customers, improve reliability, manage suppliers differently).
Linkage	Your message about "what's in it for the organization, individuals, and teams" when you realize your vision and successfully implement your strategy.	Actions you will take to assure there's "something in it for me" e.g., opportunities for organization, team, and individual growth; improved skills and employability; rewards; job security; less susceptibility to hostile takeovers.
Role	Your message about what people need to do to realize the vision and implement the strategy.	Actions you will take to help focus people's attention on their specific roles (e.g., clear goals and performance measures).
Support	Your message about how the organization will provide the resources so people can play their roles successfully.	Action you will take to make sure people have the resources they need (e.g., information, time, capital, tools, technology).

Align Communication Sources

From the above exercise, you now need to assign communication roles to each communication source. Leaders have a role to play in communicating the story. The systems have role, as do the formal media and channels. *The combined roles become a large part of your plan to connect the dots.*

Focused Message	Leadership Plan	Systems Plan	Formal Media Plan
Context: Your context message.	What leaders will say and do to tell the story.	How you will align the systems to tell the story.	What your formal media and channels will say and do.
Vision/Strategy: Your vision/ strategy message.			
Linkage: Your linkage message.			
Role: Your role message.			
Support: Your support message.			

To complete the leadership plan, look at the earlier sections of this chapter, namely leadership selection, development, and accountability. How are you going to make sure you have a steady supply of the right kinds of leaders who believe in and will work with a passion to connect the dots so their people are engaged? Is there work needed around goal clarification? What is leadership's responsibility for making sure everyone understands the goals and how they relate to them?

Then look back at Chapter 4. How can you manage what you do around the things that people say communicate the loudest, namely:

- What you take the lead on
- What you spend time on
- How well you listen
- Who and what you reward and recognize
- How you use symbolism

Do the same thing with the systems plan. Review Chapter 5. Pay particular attention to the five systems that seem to communicate the loudest, including:

- Structure
- Measurement and rewards
- Policies and procedures
- Resource allocation
- Working environment

How can they and other components of the systems infrastructure be managed to help tell the story? How can you make sure the systems aren't in conflict with the story, that they aren't encouraging people to *do* things that are incompatible with the *say*. The systems infrastructure possesses a lot of opportunities to undermine the story and your credibility as a leader.

Do the same with the formal communication media. This is usually the easiest part of the process to create and tell the story. Each formal medium should have a single charter: to communicate the story in every way it can. If a proposed article for a publication doesn't help communicate the story, it probably shouldn't be published. Except in very special circumstances, that out-of-alignment article should be rejected for publication or modified so it helps tell the story. Because the story is now so closely linked to the business strategy, the formal communication media will now be in a much better position to help implement the business strategy than they have before you made this adjustment. This can help improve the value-to-cost of the formal media.

Because huddling can be so powerful (see Chapter 6) consider this process first, before you consider elaborate formal media, especially if you are a smaller organization with limited resources. For the investment, huddling can generate more return than most any other medium. In one medium, it can help build the four engagement components: line of sight, involvement, information sharing, and rewards and recognition. And in larger organizations, it can capitalize on the use of Web-technology.

Do It

Stories start with leaders. Great leaders tell the story over and over again. Repeat! Repeat! Repeat! Then repeat it again.

Steve Case, AOL's chairman, tells the AOL vision over and over again. In *USA Today,* Kevin Maney stated: "Just so there's no chance any person on Earth could forget the message, Case says it in his speeches. He says it in AOL meetings. He says it if you ask about the weather. I'm willing to bet he says it to telemarketers who call him at home during dinner, which probably prevents them from ever calling back.[22]

That's what Tom Downs was doing at Amtrak. Everywhere he went, he told that story. He asked people, "What's the story?" He listened to others tell the story. When they told the story he was trying to tell, he told them they had it right. When they didn't, he'd gently coach them. He'd tell the story to them once again so they had it straight.

Leaders tell stories in many different ways, but they mostly tell stories with their actions—what they do. Their stories make it clear what's important and where people should focus their attention and energy.

Stay with it! It may seem difficult at first, but once you've built a communication system you can manage, it gets easier—or as easy as anything in business gets these days.

Remember, for many leaders, this isn't like going on a diet. It's more like changing your lifestyle.

Leaders at organizations like Medtronic, Hewlett-Packard, Johnson & Johnson, The Mayo Clinic, AOL, FedEx, Dell, Apple and Hallmark tell the story over and over again.

They keep the story alive!

CHAPTER 11

Find the Flaw

If you want it, measure it. If you can't measure it, forget it.

— Peter Drucker

Pete is president of a geographical division of a large telecommunication company. A few years before his call, I had worked with him, his peers, and the company's CEO to help them get aligned around their business strategy and a focused message. The project had gone well.

Pete was now on the phone with a problem and a proposed solution. What did I think of his idea?

He said he wanted to generate high levels of commitment among his 11,000 employees to the company's entire product line. People either don't know what products the company sells or they only know the products sold by their group or division, he told me. "What I'd like to do is generate their commitment to our entire product line so we have the potential of 11,000 ambassadors out there capable of selling all of our products every day," Pete said.

"Here's my idea and I'd like your thoughts."

173

"Go ahead, I'm all ears."

"What we're talking about," Pete explained, "is renting out the city's convention center and busing in all 11,000 employees. Essentially we'd shut the company down for about four hours on one day." (He said employees critical to the company's continued operation would remain on the job; their supervisors would brief them after the event.) "We're talking about having a huge rally, complete with speeches from the leadership team, bands, confetti, balloons, you name it. We'll explain that we want everyone to be knowledgeable about our entire product line so they can serve as ambassador for the whole company in (our geographic area)." He already had a rah! rah! theme and slogan for the rally.

"So what do you think? Will it work?" he asked.

I asked him how much he had budgeted for the rally and he said excluding down time for the 11,000 employees, the day would cost "several hundred thousand dollars."

I asked him one question: Do you know for sure that people aren't committed to serving as ambassadors to your entire product line because you *haven't* had a rally such as the one you're proposing?

"What do you mean?" he asked.

"Well," I explained, "you're going to spend several hundred thousand dollars to eliminate a flaw that resides somewhere in your communication system. Do you know for sure that the rally will eliminate the flaw?"

I then took him slowly through some of the areas where the flaw might be residing. I asked him if he'd looked at each of the components of engagement: line of sight; involvement; information sharing; and rewards. He said he hadn't. I asked him if he'd looked at each of the information categories and determined where people might lack information or where people were receiving mixed messages. He said he hadn't.

I told him he should very quickly analyze the communication system and identify the flaw that was preventing people from being committed to the company's product line—preventing them from serving as ambassadors. "Pete, the flaw is there," I said. "We just need to find it. I'm concerned that you would spend the kind of money you're talking about spending without first having a clear understanding of the problem."

I met with Pete and his leadership team in his offices the next week and spent some time helping them think through their dilemma.

Wisely, Pete abandoned the rally.

Based on a lot of rallies that had come before this proposed rally, the rally's outcome was predictable. Employees would come to the convention center, some annoyed that they were pulled away from important work and their concomitant deadlines, others glad they could get off work for a few hours. The rally would go as Pete envisioned. People would leave, some grumbling about having to go back to work, others cynical about the rally, and still others with a sugar buzz courtesy of all the hoopla.

The buses would take people back to their places of work. *And, nothing would change.*

Why?

1. Because Pete hadn't addressed the underlying problem—the flaw in the communication system that was preventing commitment to the company's product line.
2. Because Pete tried to solve the communication problem with an event—a *mere media solution.*
3. Because nothing else changed. Back at work, leaders in the form of directors, managers, and supervisors would say and do the same things they had before the rally. The system's infrastructure wouldn't change. Rewards, measurement, resources, structure, policies and procedures, and the environment would all remain the same.

Pete had, therefore, designed a solution—the rally—that *would guarantee people's continued lack of commitment to the product line.*

When there's a performance problem to be reckoned with, it's almost always because there is a flaw somewhere in the communication system. Either communication sources aren't communicating messages consistent with improving performance, or they're not aligned. That is, the say and do are out of sync. Or, there are content gaps. People aren't receiving information they need when they need it in one of the five information categories. If the problem centers around commitment or engagement, it usually means there's a gap in one of the four components of engagement: line of sight; involvement; information sharing; and rewards and recognition.

The leader's job is to find and remove the flaw. Communication systems are similar to manufacturing systems. If the machinery and ingredients don't change, the manufacturing system will continue to reliably produce what it's producing. If that system is producing defective products, it will continue to produce defective products until something changes.

Similarly, if the communication system's machinery and ingredients don't change, it will continue to reliably produce what it's producing. If the communication system is producing defects in the form of poor performance, it will continue to produce poor performance until someone changes the system by finding and removing the flaw that's causing the poor performance.

There are a lot of reliable tools and techniques to help us find the flaws. Each has its advantages and disadvantages. We try to draw upon those that best fit our flaw-finding needs.

Some tools are simple, the business equivalent of a blood pressure test. Others are more comprehensive, and distinguished by their analytical rigor. They're the business equivalent of a full-blown physical at the Mayo Clinic with a CAT scan thrown in for good measure.

As an example, a global manufacturer experienced a decline in several key performance indicators, including productivity, quality, and safety. The leadership team wanted specific quantitative data about the communication flaws that were causing the performance problems as well as a clear understanding of the impact various potential solutions could have on the business. They were looking for trade-offs. "If we fix A, what will we get in return?" If we fix B, what is the upside potential?"

There is a wide range of diagnostic tools available to us to uncover communication flaws. I'll highlight four.

The Engagement Index

The Engagement Index © is elegant in its simplicity. Developed by a crack Towers Perrin team led by Diane Gherson, Monica Oliver, and Doug Friedman, the index helps identify where people or groups of people lie on an engagement continuum. There are three points on the continuum: job holders, contributors, and employee owners.

Job holders meet minimal requirements and are needed to get behind-the-scenes work done.

Contributors tend to be responsive to needs. They're critical to customer satisfaction and other factors that are important to a company's success.

Employee owners think and act like owners of the business. They have high potential to influence the company's direction and outcome.

These three points on the continuum have nothing to do with position in the organization or level within the hierarchy. They reflect a person's mindset, the degree to which she is engaged, the degree to which the dots connect for her.

The index is derived from scores on a 50-item questionnaire. The questionnaire helps identify the extent to which people understand line of sight, feel involved, have the information they need when they need it, and will be rewarded or recognized for their contributions to the business—the four engagement components discussed in Chapter 2. The index also measures how well people can translate bigger-picture issues to their own behavior. The more they make that translation, the more they'll tend to act as employee owners.

The index can help an organization with finite resources improve business performance by surgically improving engagement levels within pieces of a business—functions, processes, countries, or facilities.

For instance, the Engagement Index was applied to a global pharmaceutical company that was having difficulty getting new products into the development pipeline. We discovered that there were opportunities to improve performance by improving engagement levels.

An insurance company's business is highly influenced by its claims operations and its agents, if it sells through agents. Increasing the level of engagement in these two areas might generate proportionally higher levels of performance than increasing engagement levels elsewhere, say in underwriting. In other words, the Engagement Index provides a baseline for determining where to focus the fix.

Say-Do Assessment

The say-do assessment uncovers mixed messages and their sources. It consists of a battery of questions that invites survey participants to assess the extent to which the company or its leadership *says* certain principles or values are important (e.g., quality products or low costs) and the extent to which the company actually *delivers on* those principles or values. Figure 11-1 shows the results of one page of a say-do assessment of an electric utility.

Here's what it says. Employees believe the company both says and does sound financial management, reliable service, and safety. These are the factors in the upper-right-hand box—high say, high do.

It delivers mixed messages on customer focus, effective leader-

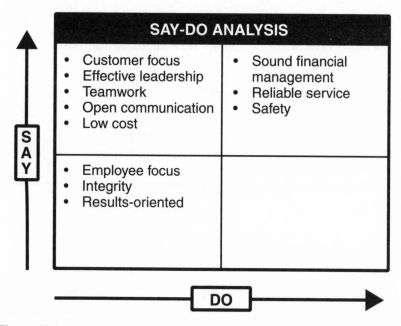

Figure 11-1.

ship, teamwork, open communication, and low cost. These are the factors in the upper-left-hand box—high say, low do.

In employees' eyes, the company neither talks about nor delivers on being employee-focused, operating with integrity, or being results-oriented. These are the principles or values in the lower-left box—low say, low do.

Performance Barrier Assessment

The performance barrier assessment identifies communication flaws that are hindering a company from achieving specific performance targets. Performance targets might include improving speed to market, building brand identity, or becoming a low-cost producer. The assessment helps uncover where communication mismanagement—or a flaw in the system—is contributing to poor performance in an area where the company must do well to compete.

- Difficulty moving approvals through the hierarchy
- Don't have enough input from customer and brand management
- Geographic and functional silos between R&D, Engineering and Chemicals restricts information-sharing and ideation process
- Sense of urgency has not successfully been communicated into the cautious culture
- Don't understand "what's in it for me" if I contribute to new product process

Figure 11-2. Results of a performance barrier assessment.

Figure 11-2 lists the results of a survey by a consumer products company that wanted to uncover communication barriers to getting new products to market quickly.

As you can see from the list, there were five key communication-related barriers to improving speed to market. With this information and the additional data a performance barrier assessment generates, a company could develop a strategy to eliminate communication as a significant barrier to an important performance target or capability that's needed to win.

Content Assessment

The content assessment does exactly what it says. It assesses the extent to which people have information they need in each of the five categories: context, vision and strategy, linkage, role, and support. A content assessment can be conducted using focus-group discussions or a written survey instrument. It also can include questions asking people what kind of information they most want more of. Here's the result of each of these assessments. (See Figures 11-3 and 11-4.)

also argue that normative data could lull a company's leadership into a sense of false security: "If our scores are better than the norm, we aren't that bad off." This can be dangerous.

In general, high-performing organizations tend to listen to both schools but lean more toward the second. They "peek" at normative data but obsess over establishing their own baselines and then improving on them. When they reach very high performance levels, norms become irrelevant to them. Only their own scores matter. To do otherwise would be the equivalent of a world-class athlete spending a lot of time trying to find out how his physical condition compares with the general population.

Companies that connect the dots best tend to measure a lot and in many ways. Communication measurement is continuous. Rather than large communication assessments every couple of years, as was the practice 10 years ago, the best companies are conducting short, quick-hit assessments that they can act on quickly. Assess, find the flaw, fix, and move on! Assess, find the flaw, fix, and move on!

The objective: Get the dots connected where they're not. Improve and improve some more. Quickly!

Every company, large or small, should be continuously assessing its communication system and identifying what's working and what's not. How are communication flaws in the system causing you to underperform? How can you get more value for your communication investment? How can you get the dots connected and keep them connected?

CHAPTER 12

Benchmarking and Best Practices

The old idea of the manager knowing a few more facts than his subordinates is nonsense; leaders share information so everyone understands the vision and contributes to its success. That's what communication is all about. And it's at the heart of managing the modern corporation.

— Jack Welch, Chairman of GE

Because the communication process is central to connecting the dots, companies want to know "Who's the best?" "From whom can we learn?" "What do these companies do that's so materially different from the also-rans?"

Business leaders often want to benchmark other companies to learn how to improve their own communication processes so they can generate increased performance. If you are new to the subject, benchmarking is "a positive, proactive process to change operations in a structured fashion to achieve superior performance," Robert C. Camp wrote in *Benchmarking, The Search for Industry Best Prac-*

tices That Leads To Superior Performance. As Camp says, benchmarking forces organizational functions "to investigate external industry best practices and incorporate those practices into their operations."

Unfortunately, there's a wrong way to benchmark communication best practices, and it has frustrated a lot of people. I don't want you, the reader, to be frustrated, so I'll describe the wrong way. Then I'll describe the right way.

First, the people doing the benchmarking contact a few leading communication consultants and people they know in the communication profession and in peer companies. From these contacts, they create a short list of companies that most people agree are known for excellent communication management.

Second, they contact the communication people inside the companies selected. They explain their project and essentially invite themselves to visit the so-called excellent companies.

Third, they visit the companies. While at the companies, they meet with senior communication people. They are taken on a tour of the company's formal communication channels. They see the publications, click on the intranet, screen a video or two and watch a business television program while it's being taped.

Fourth, they return home and are frustrated.

Everybody I've spoken with who pursued this approach came home, as they said, "empty-handed." They networked. They learned a few things about what others do. But they learned little to nothing that could be applied back home. Why?

It's because they focused on what *another* company does to communicate formally instead of focusing on what they should do to solve their communication problems. They go to the other company solution-focused instead of problem-focused. They focus on the other company, not on theirs.

In many respects, those that manage communication particularly well don't do a lot different from companies that do an average job. The inventory of possible practices, tools, techniques, processes, activities, programs, media, and initiatives is relatively finite. There simply is no *Communication Best Practices Book of Exceptional Solutions* reserved for those who can proffer the mystical best practices handshake. They just do what they do real well. They execute well in communication management just as they tend to execute well in most everything else they do.

As an example, 3M's practices aren't really that different from companies that get average scores in communication management, but the company has always valued people and innovation. 3M's leadership has always known that an avenue to innovation is a wide-open information-sharing process that fosters the creativity needed to bring new products to market. This value system nurtures the communication process. It promotes superior execution. 3M just *believes* in it. On the other hand, average companies might start a communication process or initiative, tolerate it for a while, and let it fall by the wayside. Or it may not invest the time, energy, or money needed to make the process or initiative a success. This isn't unlike success in anything else. Those who win at anything most often do so because of superior execution, not magic bullets.

It's usually a mistake to try to copy what successful organizations do or to plug into one organization's techniques that work well for another. What works well in one culture, organizational structure, industry, or particular set of operating conditions often doesn't work in another. People who've gone to Springfield, Missouri, to study SRC have learned a lot, to be sure. There's a vast inventory of practical, workable ideas that they can learn at Jack Stack's Great Game of Business seminars. But to plug Stack's know-how into their own organizations *a la* SRC is impossible. Why? First of all, they don't have Jack Stack.

Another would-be communication benchmarker visited Motorola, a company that manages communication very well. "It was all very interesting," she said. "They're great at what they do. But I came back to my office, sat down behind my desk, and had this epiphany. 'Hey,' I thought, 'they really don't do anything that's all that unique, that you can't read about in books and periodicals. They just apply the right things to what works best for their culture and business. It's not all that fancy'."

There's also not much to see when you visit these companies. Taking a tour of a communication best practices company isn't like watching M&Ms get spray painted at a Mars Inc. candy factory. It's not like going out on the body-weld assembly line at Toyota's huge Georgetown, Kentucky, manufacturing plant and watching robots weld pieces of a Camry frame together.

That's because companies that manage communication well don't rely on communication "things." They manage the communication *process*. What's done often isn't different from average companies. It's the *way* it's done.

The Correct Way to Benchmark

How, then, should you benchmark communication? Here are six steps. If you follow them closely, you'll be able to gather a lot of relevant information that will help improve your organization's performance.

1. Know thyself! Honestly answer the following questions: What are our values, especially about people? What do we believe about information sharing? What do we tend to share readily? What do we tend to keep silent about? What does that say about us? Is there a business reason to share more than we do now? Are we willing to share more than we do now?

2. Know the problem. Ask yourself the following questions: What do we need to do particularly well to win? How are we doing

at those things? Where might poor communication management (e.g., mixed messages, slow-moving or dropped information or lack of involvement) be contributing to performance problems in areas that are important to our success? Where's the flaw in the communication system? Is it in the communication sources or the communication content?

3. Know the solution. Ask yourself the following questions: What should be included in our inventory of potential actions to take to eliminate the flaw or flaws? What one or two courses of action might have the greatest impact on eliminating the flaw and improving business performance?

4. Learn from others. Ask yourself these questions: Have other parts of our organization addressed similar communication problems? Is there anything we can learn from them? How have other organizations addressed similar problems? What can be learned from them? What's the best way to study what others have done and apply it to our organization?

5. Study what others have done. Call them. Read about them. Visit them. Learn as quickly and as inexpensively as you can.

6. Fix the flaw. Implement what you learned from others, both inside and outside your organization, to improve your business. You now have *your* solution to *your* problem, which you've enriched with the experience of others.

When people study L.L. Bean, they study the things that L.L. Bean does particularly well, order processing or warehouse picking, for instance. They don't study the entire company. When companies study Toyota, they might study the company's world-class manufacturing system, not the whole company.

Similarly, if you want to benchmark communication, don't study communication at R.R. Donnelley & Sons. Study the way they use small games in the Allentown, Pennsylvania, plant to improve performance. Likewise, don't study communication at Motorola. Study how they outsource communication projects. Don't study communication at the Mayo Clinic. Study how they've organized their communication division around a professional services model that works.

Don't study communication at GTE. Study how they use business television for distance learning.

Likewise, study AT&T's communication measurement process, Allstate's communication to performance correlation research, Owens-Corning's environment of collaboration, Southwest Airlines recruiting process, or Ritz-Carlton's orientation program.

Many companies that might not otherwise make anyone's list of Best Communicating Companies do one or two things particularly well, often at a best in class level. Focusing on how someone else solved a specific problem that is similar to yours is the best way to benchmark.

Try to be as specific as you can about what you want to improve. Identify specific problems and then find specific ways to eliminate those problems. That's the key to learning from the masters. It might be more difficult to do, but it will work better for you.

Part Three:
Lessons Learned

- To reach the highest levels of performance, communication must be managed as a system. The system includes both the sources of information and content. Sources and content must work in harmony.
- When the business environment changes, the communication system needs to be adjusted. It needs to be realigned with the larger environment.
- Managing the system begins with the story we want everyone in the organization to understand. Then we tell that story through what we say and what we do, through our leadership's actions, through what systems tell people to do, and through our formal communication channels.
- The story begins with leaders. Leaders need to be selected, developed, and held accountable for connecting the dots. They need to clarify and communicate their goals, create an information-rich environment, and reinforce the story through what they say and do.
- When business performance isn't what it should be, there's often a flaw in the communication system. People receive mixed messages that confuse them and diffuse their behavior. They lack information they need to perform at their peak; they don't get the information when they need it; or they have the wrong information. It's the leader's job to find the flaw and remove it.
- Benchmarking should begin by focusing on your problem not someone else's solution.

PART FOUR

Connecting
the Dots

Connecting the dots isn't a luxury reserved for companies that have gotten everything else right. It's a process for getting everything else right. It's what helps propel the best companies to success in the first place.

So whether your company is riddled with performance problems that need eliminating or you're trying to boost your already high-performing organization one notch higher, connecting the dots can help achieve your objective.

The next two chapters draw on this book's learnings so far and apply them in a corporate environment. They represent adaptations of actual business problems companies have encountered and the solutions that were applied.

Chapter 13 demonstrates the power of putting to work the best principles that were explored in Chapter 3. With the CEO as champion, employees recognized for the value they could bring, and communication productively managed as an integrated system, the company profiled attacked a serious cost problem and used it to begin changing its culture—what it valued.

Chapter 14 harkens back to Chapters 2 and 7. It looks at what can happen when people have a clear line of sight, when they get involved, when they have gobs of decision-making information at their finger-tips, and are rewarded and recognized for their contributions.

Chapter 15 addresses one of the most violent forces that can hit a company—a merger or acquisition. Mergers and acquisitions hit companies and their people like a microburst hits a sailboat. They can knock a business down. Unless you know how to manage through such turbulent events, you and your people will experience the most frightening and debilitating times in your journey through the work world. A merger or acquisition requires triage. The ability to connect the dots will be extremely difficult. But if you want to maintain high levels of performance during a merger or acquisition, you have no choice but to try hard to get them—or keep them—connected.

Connecting the dots is hard. But when you see it happen, it can be an exciting part of your role as a leader.

CHAPTER 13

The Furniture Company

People who make a difference—who feel like they're making a difference—are partners in meeting the goals. They're not counting down the hours until it's time to go home.

— Venita McCellon-Allen,
Senior Vice President, AEP

T he president of a furniture distributor was on the phone. Bob isn't a chatty guy. He's always somewhat abrupt and to the point, a very analytical, hard-nosed businessman. But I had learned from working with him on an earlier project that Bob is attuned to people issues and how they can influence his company's performance.

Tossing aside social formalities, Bob got right to the point. "Jim, I just got a report that says we're running about $1 million in damage in our warehouse annually. Product is getting broken. Forklifts are backing into walls. It's apparently a real mess. I have no idea what's causing it, but we've got to get to the heart of it immediately."

Bob had headed the company for five years. Since becoming CEO, the $350 million company had maintained a steady 15 percent growth rate over all of his five years. The number of employees now exceeded 1300, with about 300 at corporate headquarters and in an attached central distribution center. The remaining employees were in retail stores up and down the east coast.

We agreed to meet the following week. When we did, he shared the damage report and discussed a few possible reasons for the damage. I suggested that we do three things. We'd carefully analyze any current or historical data that existed regarding inventories and the amount and nature of reported damage. We'd interview key employees, including his leadership team and warehouse employees. And we'd ask each department manager in the warehouse to report first thing every Monday morning the amount of damage in his department at the beginning of the week.

I wanted to start going after root causes as soon as possible. I knew the damage report would provide important information. I also knew the warehouse employees would shine a bright light right at the problem. (I recall the legendary poultry processor, Frank Perdue, walking me through his Salisbury, Maryland, processing plant. "See Keith over there," Perdue said, pointing to a young man on the processing line. "Keith knows his 25 square feet of space better than anyone else in this company. So when I want to know what's going on in that particular 25 square feet of space, I go ask Keith.") You learn a lot by asking the people who do the job every day.

I had requested the damage report because I wanted to start fixing the problem right away. I knew that asking warehouse department managers to count the damage every week would communicate that damage reduction was important. What you count counts. I was counting on the counting process to start to reduce damage.

Over the next week, we conducted our interviews, and I met with Bob on Friday. We were loaded with information about the problem and its causes. Here's what we told him.

The heads of sales, marketing, and operations told us their goals and incentives were tied to revenue growth. They were the first to tell us that they "had heard" that the board of directors was obsessed with becoming a billion-dollar company.

> Communication system flaws: Word was out, so to speak, that all that mattered to the board was growth. Goals and incentives communicated the importance of making the top line number—growth.

Warehouse employees told us they didn't know there was a damage problem but wouldn't be surprised. "Nobody's ever talked about it," a forklift driver told us. Nor had employees seen customer satisfaction data that we'd been given that showed an alarming decline in satisfaction. Customers complained of poor product quality and unfriendly drivers who tracked mud from their shoes onto their carpets when they delivered the furniture.

> Communication system flaws: "Nobody's ever talked about it" meant the organization's leadership hadn't communicated the importance of keeping damage and its attendant costs low. The company failed to communicate that customer satisfaction was important and was declining. It also missed an opportunity to encourage the very employees who were causing the declining numbers to identify ways to prevent further erosion and turn the numbers around.

Employees told us their supervisors pushed production only. "All they want is for us to get it out the door, a lot of it and fast," one employee said. "We hurry, we run into things, furniture gets damaged." Drivers said dispatchers and schedulers overloaded their schedules. "There's no way I can make all my calls in one day and still have a half hour for lunch. It's ridiculous," a driver told us. "We have to go in, slam the furniture together and get on to the next delivery." (When we'd walked through the warehouse, we noticed that bulletin board postings dealt with one subject—ship rates: how much product was being shipped daily and weekly.)

One employee spoke up in a focus group: "I probably shouldn't say this, but a lot of us are looking," he said.

"Looking?" we asked.

"Yeah, other jobs. This is a good crew here. A lot of companies would kill to have this bunch of guys. But this place is unreasonable." Others in the group nodded.

> Communication system flaws: The production emphasis from supervisors, dispatchers, schedulers, and bulletin boards communicated that only one thing was important: get product out the door.

A department head was first to tell us about poor quality *coming into* the warehouse. "A lot of what's coming into receiving is pretty shabby," she said.

We asked her to elaborate.

"It's like they don't care any more. The material that comes into receiving has been getting real bad. It's like they don't care about quality anymore. If they don't care, why should we care?"

We told the purchasing manager what we'd heard and he confirmed it. He said he'd "gotten the word" to keep the cost of everything down. "I've been told to put the squeeze on all of our vendors. The stuff we're getting from them now is junk. I think it's pretty shortsighted, but it's what Bob and the board want."

"Did you tell them you thought this was shortsighted?" we asked.

"You don't tell this board what to do," the purchasing manager said. "They don't want input from anyone, sometimes including Bob and his management team."

> Communication system flaws: Bob and the board communicated that the purchasing manager should cut the costs of everything.

The result of his actions communicated that quality wasn't important, indirectly reinforcing the message people in the warehouse were receiving about the singular focus on production. The board communicated that it wanted Bob, his leadership team, and the rest of the organization to comply with its wishes. They had communicated that anyone else's ideas didn't matter.

The communication system was working perfectly, that is, if perfect means that it was producing exactly what it was designed to produce: high volume, poor quality, dissatisfied customers, increasingly frustrated employees, and potentially expensive turnover, and of course, lower volume.

The communication system would continue to produce these defects as long as it was designed the way it was. To change what the communication system produced, it would need to be redesigned.

The first step in the redesign had already been put in place. By requiring warehouse department managers to report damage every Monday morning, we had begun to redesign a piece of one of the major communication sources—the measurement system. Within the first three weeks of counting damage, the cost of damage in the warehouse dropped 35 percent. But that first 35 percent represented so-called low-hanging fruit, the easiest gains to make. If we had stopped there, damage reduction might have continued but probably would have tapered off at some point, and we would only have dealt with one small piece of the communication system. That's progress, to be sure, but nothing like what could be gained from an integrated communication system that would connect the dots for everyone in the organization.

So we went to work to redesign the communication system.

Bob and the board agreed on a set of communication guidelines and a focused message, the story it wanted everyone in the organization to understand. The focused message addressed industry issues, the company's growth strategy, the importance of satisfied customers to growth, how everyone in the organization could influence the company's growth, and why it was in everyone's best interest to build the business.

The company balanced its incentives so they focused on growth *through* satisfied customers. Bob placed a temporary incentive on the warehouse damage assessment problem. If the company reduced the damage level to 2 percent of warehouse inventory, employees would share a percentage of the overall savings. It did and they did.

People throughout the company participated in workshops to help them understand the economics of the business and how they could influence business performance. Regular meetings and prominently displayed visuals reported on progress-to-date against key business drivers. Employees learned how to solve problems and used what they'd learned in their regularly scheduled meetings. The reward system was modified so everyone had an incentive for the company to meet its goals.

Bob learned a few lessons. The biggest? "Get out into the company and listen to the people who do real work. If I'd done that sooner, I could have caught this mess a lot sooner."

Or maybe avoided it altogether.

CHAPTER 14

The Oil Company

*You can't hire millions of people, pay yourself
a lot of money, have a golden parachute, and
then say, "trust me."*

— Dermot Dunphy, CEO of Sealed Air

Nobody really *buys* communication, anymore than they *buy* gasoline. Plenty of times, I've gotten a little excited about buying a new car or a shirt or pair of running shoes. But I've never gotten up at the crack of dawn and shouted, "Hey, I'm really looking forward to stopping by the gas station and buying some new gas."

People don't buy gas. They buy the ability to get somewhere. Getting where you want to go makes the gasoline purchase necessary.

It's the same with communication. I've never heard a client get excited about investing in communication. But I've heard plenty of them spend a lot of time, energy, and money improving communication so they can get what they're really after—growth, earnings, better costs, productivity, quality, service, or speed.

Oil companies know you don't crave buying gasoline. They know that you're only there so you can keep your car moving down the street. Yet they've gotten really smart about grabbing a little larger share of your pocketbook while they've got you.

It's called the convenience store, or mini-mart. They attach themselves to gas stations. They sell anything from soft drinks, snacks, newspapers, magazines, candy, and water to lottery tickets, fire logs, ice scrapers, gas treatment, toothpaste, and sunglasses.

If you lead a big company, you can understand the complexity of managing a lot of these convenience stores throughout a country or geographic territory. If you lead a smaller organization, any one of these mini-marts is really a small business with small business problems. They only employ seven or eight people, with no more than two or three working at any one time.

A lot of transactions take place in these convenience stores. The customer pays for her gas, sandwich, and newspaper. The clerk behind the counter takes her money, puts it into the cash register, and gives her any change she's owed. When customers aren't in the store, employees mop the floor, clean the restrooms, or replace a light bulb that burned out earlier in the day.

At first, these tasks seem relatively routine. There's not a whole lot of discretionary effort associated with them—unless, that is, the convenience store changes the focus of work from being transaction-based to being values-based, putting its focus on customer relationships.

One company did just that. They built line of sight. They got employees involved in improving the business. They tied rewards and recognition to results. And they used communication to build an information-rich environment. They connected the dots.

The company started by explaining to its store managers how to teach their people the business of the business. The chart shown in Figure 14-1 is similar to the one it used to explain how the company made money and how employees could help the company make more money.

In one of the convenience stores, a store manager started by teach-

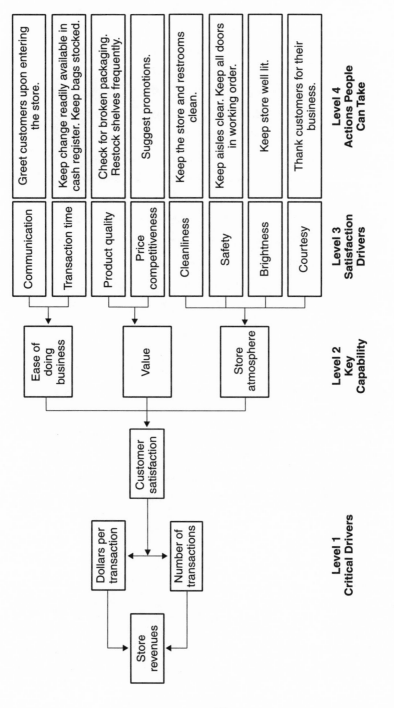

Figure 14-1. Teaching employees the business of the business.

ing his people that store revenues were driven by the number of customer transactions each day and the amount of those transactions. When the number of transactions and the amount of each transaction increases, revenues will increase, he explained.

Then the manager explained that both tend to increase when one thing happens, i.e., when customers are happy. So if there was one thing his team needed to do, it was to make customers happy.

But not just any old happy. There are certain things customers value more than others. They want to come into the store, transact their business, and get out easily and quickly—ease of business. They also want value for their money and a positive store atmosphere. To the customer, a positive store atmosphere is one that's clean, safe, bright, and where employees are courteous. If they can have these four things, they're happy, come to the store more often, and probably buy more each time. Revenues go up. The manager conveyed all this to his employees

Then the store manager involved his people in identifying the kinds of work they could do to increase the number of satisfied customers who, in turn, would drive revenues up. His team created a list of activities. It's on the far right side of Figure 14-1.

"But," the team asked, "what happens when we do all these things? Doing all these things means more work. What's in it for us?"

To which the store manager answered, "Instead of paying you a flat amount every week, your pay will be determined partly on how well we do. If our store revenues go up and our store costs stay low, we'll make more money and have more to go around. A percentage of the increase will find its way into your pockets." He explained the plan in detail.

Of course, this sounded good to people who had been paid an hourly wage, paid just for showing up, not for the results they produced. They were ready to sign up. "But," they said, "if we have a stake in this game, then we need to make sure you give us the information and resources to improve the business. We need to know which promotions we need to focus on. We need to know how we're doing against our revenue goals. We need a lot of information. We also need the tools to keep the place up. If the toilets get clogged or break down, we have to be able to fix them or customers won't be happy. They'll buy less and that comes out of our pockets."

They added something else: "You need to listen to us when we have suggestions for making customers happier. We're here every day. We hear what they ask for, gripe about, say they don't want. When we tell you what's on the customers' minds, you need to listen to us. We're not going to ask for an arm and a leg. We know the improvements have to create a gain, not a drain."

The store manager liked what he was hearing, promised his team a steady flow of information to help them do their work, and promised he'd listen. "That doesn't mean we can or will do everything you ask for, but if you have an idea that I decide not to go with, I owe you an explanation as to why," the store manager told them.

Over time, the team's business savvy increased. At first, some of their suggestions were a little off base. Some were way off-base. But the store manager was patient. He continued to teach the business of the business. He continued to supply a lot of information so people could make the right decisions and do the right things to satisfy customers. He got people together to solve specific store problems. One month, the store hit a particularly high revenue target while costs remained low. The manager called his team together, packed them up in his van, and drove them to a local pizza restaurant where they spent an evening celebrating. At the end of the evening, the team got bold and set an even higher target for the next month. If they hit it, they said, they'd take the manager to dinner at his favorite restaurant. They did and the manager liked it.

If you were to ask employees who had gone through this process what business they are in, they would tell you they're in the customer satisfaction business. A year ago, they would have told you they work at a service station down the street.

Customers like the place better than the station across the street. "They're really great," one customer said. "They treat you like they care. They treat us like family when we go in for coffee on the way to work."

Revenues have gone up. So have the profits.

"As long as their share of our gain is a percentage of the overall gain, I'd like to make them all millionaires," the store manager said. "I know I'll never be able to do that with this one station, but it's fun trying."

Connecting the dots is profitable, and it can be fun.

CHAPTER 15

Earthshaking Events

Buying is fun; merging is hell.

— Group vice president of an
acquiring company

I f linking people to strategy represents a major challenge during
normal times—whatever normal is these days—creating the linkage during and after a merger or acquisition raises the challenge
exponentially.

Few events in the corporate life cycle jolt an organization as much.
Managing through them is the equivalent of a high-wire balancing
act. For people inside the organization, they're a reliable source of
anxiety and uncertainty, and with good reason. The odds of success
are usually less than even.

Various studies have concluded that from one-third to one-half of
all acquisitions in the Unites States are subsequently divested. A Simon
School of Business study at the University of Rochester showed, not
surprisingly, that the acquiring company suffers immediately after the
transaction, with its stock falling an average of 4 percent, adjusted for
market movement.

During mergers or acquisitions, the communication system possesses the extraordinary power to facilitate or impede the process. Consider a recent example.

Shortly after Citicorp and Travelers Group merged, *The Wall Street Journal* ran a lengthy article bearing the headline "How a New Financial Giant Struggles With Its Message."

The story quoted employees in both organizations. They said company leaders were sending "confusing signals about everything from the meaning of the word *integrate* to whether they will work on the same premises under a new brand name."

"Every executive you talk to—they think it's going one way—and then you hear it's going another way," the *Journal* quoted one Citigroup manager as saying.

Mergers and acquisitions and related traumatic events, such as restructuring, downsizing, and divestitures, throw a wrench into an already difficult-to-manage communication process. Everyone in both companies is quickly slapped with a new range of feelings and emotions—shock, denial, confusion, anxiety, resignation, anger, frustration, and fear.

People feel blindsided and sold out. The secretiveness with which the leadership usually negotiates the event makes employees wonder if the leaders can be counted on to be forthright and trusted in the future. One employee I talked to during an acquisition said she felt as though her parents had just sold her to new parents she didn't even know. "It's like, who are these people who are now in command of my life?"

How can people who were not involved in the M&A process and who feel sold out to new parents have any ownership in the new deal? How can an environment stewing with these emotions produce high performance? How can people perform at their peak when they're hanging around water coolers and coffee rooms asking questions like What have you heard?; What's the latest?; and What's going on?—all with a single-minded but often unspoken focus on "me."

People become restless. They want and need more information.

as afterthought.) These are not the comments of leaders who value their people.

Contrast this with the case of one of the world's leading industrial companies, which has worked hard to develop a documented communication process that is integrated with the entire M&A process. "We think there's a tremendous opportunity for gaining competitive advantage and for creating value if we can eliminate communication as a barrier to merger implementation," the company's head of communication told me. "If we're batting .300 and know that a major reason why these things fail is poor communication, we've got to improve our batting average by better managing what causes them to fail. We're not there yet, but this is where we're headed."

Many companies are masters at merger integration communication. Most aren't, however. Most communication "strategies" that *are* developed are no more than formal media plans that rely on a memo or two and a glitzy intranet site. The communication comes across as: "Oh, and by the way, we wanted to let you know that you were sold yesterday. Don't worry, nothing will change. We don't have a lot more to tell you now, but when we do, we will. Blah, Blah, Blah."

You can't manage a merger or acquisition successfully with only a media or formal channels strategy. If you try, you'll fail. Guaranteed!

You must have an integrated communication strategy, a strategy that manages the entire communication system, not just one piece of it.

The goal of the communication strategy during a merger or acquisition is similar to the goal of a communication strategy any other time: to maintain or improve business performance. During a merger or acquisition, though, different forces are at work, and a different response is required.

To use another sailing metaphor, the sailboat and skipper are the same, regardless of conditions. The number of options the skipper has to sail the boat is the same, regardless of conditions. But it's a lot more difficult to sail a sailboat well in a 60-knot wind than it is in a 15-knot wind. Imagine everyday business as a 15-knot wind. Now, out of nowhere comes a 60-knot squall that slams into the side of your boat. That's the equivalent of a merger or acquisition. Managing the communication system, getting it under control and keeping it there, is much harder during a merger or acquisition.

Figure 15-1 depicts part of what occurs during a merger or acquisition.

In the chart, A represents that point in time when the initial merger or acquisition announcement is made. The descending band represents descending productivity and performance as people experience an assortment of emotions. A is that vulnerable point at which whatever dots *are* connected can begin to disconnect.

B is the productivity pit. Productivity falls to the lowest that it will be during the merger integration process.

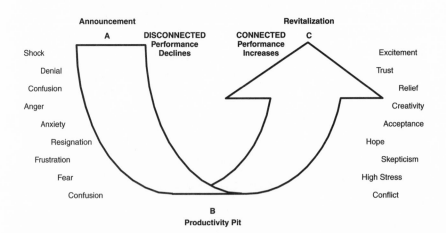

Figure 15-1.

Between B and C, the band begins to rise as the dots start to connect or reconnect. Emotions shift from negative to positive, albeit cau-
tiously at first.

C represents revitalization. The dots are connected. The organization has regained its productivity and performance. Smoother sailing
returns.

The objective of an internal communication strategy built around
merger integration is to keep the time between A and C as short as
possible and the line between A and B as shallow as possible.

There will always be some amount of time between A and C. It's
unavoidable. But although you can't stop the wind, you *can* manage
the sails. If you manage the communication process well, you can
truncate the time line.

Similarly, productivity and performance will decline after any
merger or acquisition announcement, no matter how well you manage communication. Nevertheless, you can reduce the degree of the
decline if you manage it well.

Simply put, when you're managing communication during a
merger or acquisition, you're trying to keep productivity and performance as high as possible throughout the process. Everything you do
should be focused on getting to C as quickly and as effectively as you
can.

When communication is managed well during a merger, it looks
like A in Figure 15-2. When it's managed poorly, it looks like B.

The first step in designing a merger integration communication
strategy is to establish objectives for the overall effort. One client, for
example, agreed on five objectives that they wanted to achieve during
an acquisition. They wanted their objectives to relate to the acquisition itself as well as "when this is all over." Here's what they wanted
to do:

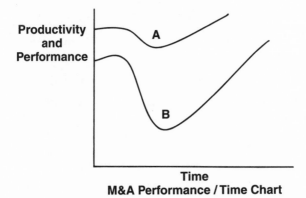

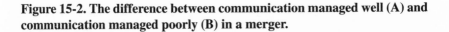

Time
M&A Performance / Time Chart

Figure 15-2. The difference between communication managed well (A) and communication managed poorly (B) in a merger.

- To maintain individual, team, and organizational performance in both companies.
- To build leadership credibility (a tall order during M&A activity, but this client had a leadership credibility problem that they felt needed to be addressed).
- To teach members of the leadership team communication skills that would be useful on an ongoing basis.
- To create a new performance-based communication process that would be in place after the acquisition.
- To signal the new organization's people values as they moved forward.

Building a merger and acquisition communication strategy is similar to building a communication strategy at any other time, just as the fundamentals of sailing a boat are the same whether you're in 10 knots of wind or a storm.

Phase 1: Making Plans

During the first phase, you should address the preannouncement issues and plan for the actual announcement.

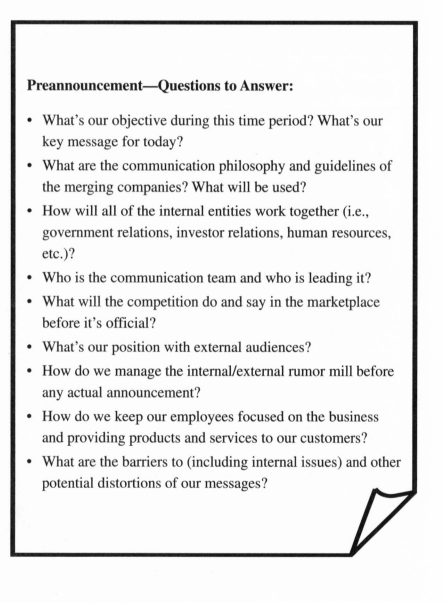

Preannouncement—Questions to Answer:

- What's our objective during this time period? What's our key message for today?
- What are the communication philosophy and guidelines of the merging companies? What will be used?
- How will all of the internal entities work together (i.e., government relations, investor relations, human resources, etc.)?
- Who is the communication team and who is leading it?
- What will the competition do and say in the marketplace before it's official?
- What's our position with external audiences?
- How do we manage the internal/external rumor mill before any actual announcement?
- How do we keep our employees focused on the business and providing products and services to our customers?
- What are the barriers to (including internal issues) and other potential distortions of our messages?

When Planning the Announcement—Questions to Answer:

- What are our objectives? What are our key messages? Are those messages aligned inside and outside the organizations?
- What's the timing? How much advance notice will we have?
- How many facilities and locations do we need to reach?
- Are there geographical or time zone issues?
- What's the method to reach audiences (press conferences, press releases, face-to-face meetings, internal news bulletins, business TV)?
- Who is doing what? Do we have enough arms and legs to cover all the bases?
- What's the detailed communication plan? Is it integrated across groups?
- Are there any new barriers or other developments we need to factor into our planning?
- What's going to happen immediately after the announcement? Who will do what follow-up communication and when?
- How will we assess the climate after measurement?
- How are we going to measure success?

Phase 2: Making It Happen

During the second phase, you should concentrate on the announcement and on establishing a pattern for the new company.

To Manage the Announcement—Questions to Answer:

- Are our objectives clear?
- Do both organizations agree on the communication philosophy and policy guidelines?
- Are we ready to execute our plan?
- Are there any other major news events (internally or externally) that will distract from our news?
- Did we meet our success criteria?

Immediately Following the Announcement— Questions to Answer:

- What groups do we need to stabilize immediately?
- Where do we need to focus our attention to keep performance high?
- Who are the crucial, at-risk groups that need immediate attention?
- What's the external world saying about our news and how does that information get translated internally?
- How do we make sure our "say communication" and our "do communication" are aligned?
- How do we handle communicating the mechanics of the news (leadership change implications, workforce reductions, new way of doing business, etc.)?
- Who are the leaders in the new organization? What are their communication roles and action plans?

Direction-Setting—Questions to Answer:

- What is the vision and business strategy for the new organization?
- How will communication be managed in the new organization?
- What is "the story," the set of focused messages for the company and for each business unit?
- How are we going to keep the momentum going (or start it)?

Key Communication Issues—Questions to Answer:

- How can communication help focus people on business targets (e.g., the sales force on customer satisfaction, or HR on program development and organizational support)?
- What is the integrated communication strategy for leadership, infrastructure, and formal channels on media?
- What works best in each culture to share information, gather information, and change behavior?
- What resources are needed to support communication at a companywide level and in each business unit?
- When will different changes affect people? How will the company assess the effects of those changes and respond?
- How will we maintain an ongoing pulse of the company so we know what information needs are and aren't being met?

Phase 3: Making It Work

During this final phase, the company is creating systems for the future.

Leadership Actions—Questions to Answer:

- How will leaders sustain (and reinforce) the leadership style that succeeded in the integration—and avoid repeating mistakes?
- What steps do leaders and the company need to take to avoid falling back into the old ways?
- How often will the leadership team assess the environment and revisit the vision, strategy, and the story?
- How are we going to win the hearts and minds of our employees?

Sailing a sailboat for maximum efficiency in a 15- to 20-knot breeze requires knowledge and skill. But when the boat gets hit abeam by a microburst (sailors call it *white wind*) that can knock a boat down, you very quickly have a different set of circumstances to manage.

It bears repeating: you can't adjust the wind, but you can manage the sails. Managing communication to connect the dots during a merger is difficult. But if you remember and pursue the following nine guidelines, you'll be way ahead of most leaders who negotiate through the microburst of a merger or acquisition.

1. Your goal in managing communication effectively during a merger is to keep performance as high as possible.

2. The leadership must agree on what it will and will not share. Agreeing on a leadership communication game plan or philosophy early will help avoid missteps, continual false starts, and information-sharing delays.

3. Create a communication strategy as soon as possible. Make sure it's integrated and includes your key stakeholders: customers, employees, investors, and suppliers. Also consider members of the communities in which you operate and regulatory groups.

4. Don't fall into the activity trap. Make sure you manage both *say* communication and *do* communication. Leadership style and behavior, the system's infrastructure, and formal media must communicate a single story, a focused message.

5. Communication is multidirectional, not just top-down. Ongoing listening and pulse-taking need to be key strategy components so your communication implementation can be as flexible and agile as possible.

6. If you have a well-managed communication process in place, use it. If you don't, use the merger communication effort as an opportunity to build one.

7. Focus on groups of people that have the greatest influence on business performance.
8. Tell the truth, even if it means acknowledging you have information that can't be shared at that point in time.
9. Maintain your credibility throughout the process; it's the core to successful communication and to keeping performance high.

Part Four: Lessons Learned

- Connecting the dots is for companies that are seriously underperforming. It's also for great companies that want to take performance to the next level.
- It's the foundation for managing through turbulent times, culture change, and earthshaking events like mergers and acquisitions.
- During any major change event, the objective is to manage communication to keep performance as high as possible—both through and after the event.

Starting Over

CHAPTER 16

Starting Over

You start playing a role that the corporate culture and the general culture expect you to play. And suddenly you're thinking that you've got it all figured out, when all you've got is hubris.

— Paul Wieand, founder of Advanced
Emotional Intelligence and former CEO
of Independence Bancorp

Dana Herbert turned a company around. He started by turning the people in his company around. Well, that's not entirely correct. Dana Herbert started by turning himself around.

"I got a real rude awakening one day," as he tells the story. "I learned I wasn't the hot-shot leader I thought I was. It hurt like hell!"

Herbert rose quickly at fast-growing Cosine, Inc. Cosine is a $1 billion manufacturer of telecommunications equipment that employs nearly 5000 people in 16 locations throughout the Midwest. At 35, Herbert became CEO. Three years later, the company's stock was in a death spiral, and Herbert told his board that the company wouldn't pay a dividend for the first time in its 20-year history.

Three weeks later, Gill Gillespie, Herbert's friend and a board member, gave him bad news.

"Gill was straight with me," Herbert recounted. "He told me the board was losing its patience with the company's performance and with my leadership. I started to trot out 10 reasons why the company wasn't performing but he wouldn't hear it. He said the board was tired of excuses, that performance was all that counted."

Herbert says he went home and stewed. He couldn't sleep. He got up early the next morning and called Marven James. James was a friend of Herbert's father and had had a stellar career running a global pharmaceutical company. He was recognized throughout the business community as a forward-thinking leader, a leader's leader, as the business press called him.

"Marven listened a long time," Herbert said. "Didn't evaluate, just listened. Then, like a big brother or father, told me what I needed to do. 'Get in touch with your people. Get in touch with your leadership team. Get to the root of the problem. Fix the company.' It was real simple. I understood what he meant. Believe it or not, I was energized!"

Herbert scheduled meetings with employees throughout the company. He went to all 16 facilities in a month.

"I spent a lot of time listening," Herbert recounted. "Part of my problem was that I'd been doing too much of the talking and not a lot of the listening."

Herbert met with employees at each facility. "At first, they didn't open up. They just sort of looked down and away from me. I couldn't tell who was the most uncomfortable, them or me.

"I kept asking and asking and pretty soon they started answering, maybe just to get rid of me. I don't know. In one visit to a Kansas operation, I got 27 different ideas on how to improve the company.

Now, some of those ideas were pretty farfetched. But some were really good, too. I learned something about all those crazy ideas. I learned our folks didn't know much about our business, why we do what we do, what we have to do to grow. To me, that meant we'd done a lousy job of informing them about the company and what makes it work. We hadn't helped them improve the quality of their ideas. That wasn't *their* fault. It was our—*my*—fault," he admitted.

After meeting with employees for a month, Herbert went back to his office and assembled his leadership team. They met for three days at a corporate training facility.

"I began by talking about the company and its history of growth and success. I talked about some of the successes we'd created together.

"But then I told them: 'that was then; this is now. What worked in the past won't work in the future because the environment has changed. Technology and the regulatory environment have changed the game. We've got to play a new game under different rules. If we keep doing what we're doing, we'll keep getting what we're getting. The shareholders don't want that. I don't want that. And I know you don't want that.' I told them about my meetings with employees, that our people had lost confidence in us. 'I don't think they trust us to run this business. They don't think we know how to run a company,' I told them. I said we had to change and the change had to begin with me.

"I told them the entire turnaround was going to rest on us, the leaders of this company, and our people, the only people in the world who, by the actions they took and didn't take, could help turn this ship around.

"'We're starting over,' I said.

"Some were with me from the get-go. I could tell from their eyes that some wanted to be with me but were skeptical. Sort of: 'Is this guy really serious?' About a third sat there with their arms folded. They were the outliers. They weren't buying it.

"We worked for three solid days. First, we agreed on our business strategy and goals. That was relatively easy because we'd gone over all that during our planning process that had just ended. Strategy wasn't the problem. It was execution."

Herbert turned his attention to the people issue that his friend James had recommended. "I told them what I'd found during my visits, that our people were uninformed and disengaged. But they had told me they cared about the company, they wanted to see us succeed, and they were willing to do what they could to help us. After all, their jobs were at stake. 'Our highest priority,' I told them, 'is to focus on our own leadership and our own people. The common thread between the two is communication. We've got to open this place up, listen better to each other, and learn to trust one another. People who don't trust each other don't commit to each others' goals. How can we expect uninformed people to beat the other guy if the other guy is working from a base of knowledgeable employees?' I asked.

"I was still getting some folded arms and skeptical looks, sort of like when people look at you that funny way when they look over their glasses. But I laid it on the line: 'Either be part of the problem or part of the solution.'

"We talked a lot about our relationship with each other and our people. What should individual employees expect from the larger team, and what should the whole team expect from each individual? In the end, we were discussing our contract with each other. My folks hadn't thought about some of these issues before, and I think it made a few of them uncomfortable—maybe too touchy-feely. But we had to do it if we were going to engage our people. We needed their hearts as well as their minds. And from what I've read and experienced in my own career, you get to people's minds differently than you get to their hearts. We have a lot of engineers in our industry and in the company. They have a little trouble with that softer stuff."

Herbert and his team agreed that communication needed to improve, but when it came time to agree on what should and shouldn't be communicated, they got bogged down. "That's when I learned that these people were coming from some really different places. Man, I'll tell you, some said 'tell them everything,' while the doubters were coming from the old military 'tell 'em what they need to know and that's all' philosophy. They're just afraid of giving up power. They think they've earned the right to hoard information, that if their people get it, it'll make them look stupid or something. We had some real antiquated thinking to deal with."

At the end of the second day, Herbert and his team had agreed on a series of statements about how they'd think about communication going forward. "But I knew that getting there would be like pulling teeth," Herbert told me.

Herbert and his team crafted the policy in Figure 16-1.

"I thought that policy was pretty ambitious because it was such a departure from what we'd been doing," Herbert told me. "I don't think my folks realized how ambitious it was until they had to do it.

"On the last day, we talked about leadership, what we expected of ourselves and others in leadership positions. We talked about holding each other accountable, that when someone slipped back into the old way of acting, we had a responsibility as individuals and as a group to call him on it. 'Be civil about it,' I told them, 'but call the guy on it if he slips backward.' (Herbert's team was all male.)

"Then, I said we needed to hold each other accountable in the pocketbook," Herbert said. "That got their attention.

"'What do you mean?' Dale asked. He was the head of manufacturing.

"'I mean that if we lead our people well, if we build a healthier environment, we'll get paid more than if we don't. We should create an incentive around it. Our total incentive should be based on creating this new environment *and* on hitting our financial goals.

"'How much do you have in mind?' Dale asked again.

Cosine Communication Policy

- Communicate what we know when we know it and move information quickly and accurately throughout the company.
- Clearly and accurately communicate our goals so that everyone has a clear understanding of what we must do to help achieve them.
- Get everyone in the business involved in the business.
- Recognize that communication is multidirectional and that listening is an important part of communicating.
- Never mislead anyone. If any communication misleads, we will correct it.
- Recognize that communication is everyone's responsibility.
- Assure that all communication reflects and respects everyone's rights.
- Treat each other as adults who are capable of assimilating both good and bad news.
- Develop our people's communication skills.
- Measure communication success through results achieved, not by the number of communication activities that occur.
- Lead by example.
- Make sure the whole company walks the talk.

Figure 16-1. A model policy checklist for reinventing the communication function.

"'I was thinking about 20 percent of our total bonus would be on living by these new values of open communication and trust.'

"'How are we going to measure it?' Dale asked again.

"I told him we'd ask our employees to evaluate us. And we'd evaluate each other on how well we were doing. We'd use a simple questionnaire that would get employee opinions of how well we were doing. I said I hadn't worked out the details but that it seemed to me that our own group and our employees would be the best judges of how we were doing.

"Dale exploded, said that was a bunch of BS, and closed up for the rest of the meeting. He didn't even look at me the rest of the day.

"But the others saw I was intent, saw that I wasn't going to back down from Dale, who's always tried to bully his way through life, so they consented. Eighty percent on the financials; 20 percent on building openness and trust. I thought that was pretty good for starters."

Herbert told his team that he wanted to introduce them to someone Gill Gillespie had recommended to him. He worked with leadership teams to build their leadership skills. He worked out of a small firm in Wilmington, Delaware. He wanted to invite him to their next meeting. Most of the group was enthusiastic. "Hey, if there's money on the table over this issue, I want all the coaching I can get," Pete, the head of engineering, told the group.

"There was some nervous laughter after Pete said what he said," Herbert told me. "I think it was laughter of doubt."

Before adjourning, Herbert and his team created a set of messages that they would begin communicating to everyone in the company. "We agreed among ourselves on a simple, straightforward story that everyone in the company needed to understand. It talked about the regulatory and economic environment, what we were trying to become in our marketplace, our strategy for getting there, all of that. It also talked about the importance of every person at Cosine and the role each of us needed to play to make this work. It talked about the good things that would come to us if we made the company great again. It said we were going to do our best—despite financial constraints—to give them what they needed to be the best they could be at what they did.

"It was a pretty compelling statement. But, you know, we got bogged down about every 15 minutes. Petty stuff. Commas and periods kind of stuff. We also got bogged down in what we meant when we said certain things, so I put each statement on a flip chart page and pinned it to the wall, sort of like pictures hung around the room. Each 'picture' had a piece of the overall story we wanted to tell our people.

"Then I asked each person on the team to walk around the room. 'Just write on each piece of paper what you think that particular statement says we should do. That is, if we say what's on the paper, what do we need to do to match our words with our actions?' I called it the museum tour. They had some fun with it. Some of the things that they wrote down were pretty ambitious. Some weren't ambitious enough. Some were downright irreverent. But they had fun with it.

"We then went through the pages and agreed on what each statement meant in terms of action. We made a list of all the action items. We called it our Alignment Plan—the things we had to do to align what we said with what we did.

"The group agreed that they would begin a series of communication meetings with their people and we'd complete all our meetings in three weeks. Some said that wasn't enough time and I said we needed to learn how to do it even faster," Herbert said. "I told them three weeks is a long time in today's business world."

After three days, the group adjourned and began meeting with employees in every business unit and function of the company. Herbert took the lead. He met with employees in every location.

"Some of the guys were doing a great job," he said. "You can guess who they were. They were the ones who were with me from the get-go. The ones with the folded arms were the worst. They either did a lousy job or simply weren't doing it."

At the end of three weeks, Herbert went out into the manufacturing plant near corporate headquarters and asked employees about the meetings.

"They just gave me blank stares," Herbert recounted. 'What meetings?' they asked."

Herbert called his mentor, Gill Gillespie, and told him about the outliers, the ones who weren't coming along, especially Dale. "Gill told me I had to balance patience and impatience. He said, 'Give them direction. Make sure they understand it. Give them the coaching they need. But you've got to hold them accountable. The consequences for those who are doing a good job must be different from the consequences for those doing a poor job. If you don't deal with the ones who aren't coming along, you're merely sanctioning what they're doing. You are, in effect, communicating that what they're doing is okay. You can't afford that, Dana,' he told me. He was very firm about that."

"Gill also told me that sometimes, to prove a point, you've got to take strong action, symbolically demonstrate that you're serious," Herbert told me.

Two weeks later, Dana fired Dale. "He continued to be the worst of the bunch, out and out defying me. I terminated Dale in a dignified way, but I didn't attempt to hide why I did it. I told our leadership team, 'If you're not going to help us start over and turn this company around, you have no place on this team. Turning this company around means engaging your people, creating an environment of openness and trust, and getting results. There will be no exceptions,' I told them. They got the message. Firing Dale had a big impact on them. I think they agreed Dale had to go and were relieved that I did what I did.

"Our meetings around the company surfaced thousands of places where we weren't walking the talk. We were asking people to do things without the information they needed to do them right, and we were sending a whole lot of mixed messages. We made notes of what they said and added it to our Alignment Plan."

Over the next year, Herbert pushed forward with his ambitious plan.

The company provided business literacy to every employee, using computer-simulation games.

"We put our marketing, engineering, and manufacturing people together in those classes," Herbert said. " Before you knew it, they'd taken off their marketing hats or engineering hats or manufacturing hats. They were working together to improve the balance sheet. That's one thing I've learned about getting everyone focused on the numbers. The balance sheet, cash flow statement, and income statement remove functional silos. They create a common language. People began to work for the company, not just their own departments."

The company got employees involved in the planning process. "Hey," Herbert said. "We used to do all the planning in the executive conference room. But our people always are the ones to deliver. We never asked them what they thought. Now we show them our projections, based on sales force input, and our required growth goals, and then ask our people whether they can hit the targets. If they say they can't, we ask them what they need to hit the target. Then we decide whether the targets are reachable."

Cosine began sharing customer satisfaction information with everyone in the company. They put in a bonus plan for everyone. "It was tied to reaching certain goals that they could influence," Herbert explained. "Where we spotted numbers that were getting out of kilter, we put a special bonus or game on it," Herbert said. "For instance, we saw workers' compensation claims costs rising, so we put a game on it. Get workers' comp down and we'll celebrate."

They also got everyone in the company involved in regular meetings that focused on forecasts, avoiding future problems, and eliminating current ones. "We do a lot of problem-solving in these meetings," Herbert told me. "We use up a lot of flip charts. We also use these meetings to recognize people and celebrate successes and what I call 'nice tries.' I created a 'nice-try fund.' When someone really stretches and puts in a lot of time and effort, but for some reason the project doesn't work out, I dip into the nice-try fund, give that person or persons who tried a chunk of change, and tell them to keep trying. That's a big motivator. It says we're serious about stretching."

Herbert read *The Visual Factory: Building Participation Through Shared Information.** "I was struck by how easy it would be to get everyone in the company focused on the same goals just by posting visuals that showed our targets and how we were doing against them. It's a constant reminder that helps keep people focused," he said.

All that started two years ago. Driving up to Cosine's entrance recently, I could sense the change. The parking lot was cleaner, lines freshly painted. The front lawn was nicely manicured. Inside the front door, the former, seemingly bored receptionist had been replaced with a bubbly young woman whose perkiness was contagious. She introduced herself as Sonya.

"Go right ahead, Jim; Dana's expecting you," the receptionist said. "Straight up those stairs there, through the glass doors, and he'll be sitting on the left."

Jim? Dana? Back in the old days, it was Mr. This and Mr. That. Stuffy! The informality is so nice, breaks down barriers, I thought.

Up five stairs and through the glass doors, just as Sonya had said, there was Herbert sitting in a sport shirt and slacks with a group of people, laughing, obviously enjoying himself. He jumped up, grabbed my hand, shook it, and quickly introduced me to the others in the room. "This is a new product team that's been slaving over flip charts for the past three weeks," Herbert explained. "They've come up with a great new line extension. They're about 80 percent convinced it will

*By Michael Greif, Productivity Press, 1991.

be a big hit. I asked them what we should do. They said 'go for it,' and we are. Should be fun."

The new product team said their good-byes and Herbert offered to show me the changes that had taken place in the past two years.

The informality that had come to prevail in the company continued to stand out. Lots of dark wood offices had been replaced by cubicles and team meeting areas. Technology everywhere. "You can't find a place in this building that's more than 25 feet from a place where you could plug in your laptop and modem," Herbert bragged.

I watched people as we approached. What a change, I thought. Two years ago, these folks were looking down and away from their CEO. Now they see him and their eyes sparkle. "Hey Carol, how'd your Dad make out?" Herbert shouted at a young woman across the room. "Hi, Dana, he's doing great. Thanks for asking."

Through some glass doors and into a large room. Across the wall near the ceiling were electronic banners with lots of codes and numbers. Thirty or forty people working phones. Three groups of people huddled, obviously working some flip charts. One group breaks, high fives all around. Back to work.

"This is our call center. All those codes and numbers are keeping track of the number of people who're calling, the average wait time, the number of, God forbid, dropped calls," Herbert said. "Those teams over there," Herbert continued, pointing to two huddles, "they're either working out a problem they've encountered, or they're reviewing financial forecasts. Could be either. We're adamant about getting to the root of a problem immediately. 'Don't let it fester. Don't let it do bad things more than once. Make it go away fast,' we say around here."

We walked on down the hall, through a back corridor and down some steps into a bright room filled with machines, and lab equipment. It looked like research and development and it was. People were sitting with their chairs formed in a circle, one group member calling out numbers. I asked Herbert what they were doing. "They're getting ready for tomorrow's huddle. They're going over the financials for their area, addressing any variances, coming up with explanations about the numbers. One of them, probably Sandra over there in the green blouse, will report on behalf of the team tomorrow. Every department will have one of these huddles sometime today to get ready for tomorrow. It only takes 15 to 20 minutes because everyone's on top of the numbers. It's the way we run this business. It helps us avoid problems in the first place. And it helps us make sure we don't encounter any problem twice. Everyone helps run the business. Eighty percent of their job is to run the business. Twenty percent is to supply skills and knowledge."

We passed out the back door, down some steps, across a parking lot and into another building, obviously manufacturing, where circuit boards were being built.

A huge red and white banner overhead announced "WE WON!" Another banner declared "GO FOR 200."

"What's that all about?" I asked Herbert.

"They've just celebrated 100,000 hours without a lost-time accident," Herbert explained. "A year and a half ago a lot of people were getting hurt out here, backs, sprains, and strains. Nothing serious, but it was stuff that, number one, hurt people, and number two, was costing the company money. Workers' compensation costs were skyrocketing. So the team out here put a game on reducing lost-time accidents. The game: If they hit 100,000 hours without a lost-time accident, we'd have a party for the whole company: spouses, friends, children, everybody. They hit 100,000 hours and we had our party last Friday night after work. Everybody loved it. Manufacturing people were seen as the heroes because they were the ones who got those costs under control for the whole company. So we celebrated them. They were the company's heroes that day."

I pointed out that Herbert and Cosine seemed to have a lot to celebrate.

"Absolutely," Herbert said. "We all have a lot to celebrate. Customers love us. Our revenues are up. Earnings are up. Shareholders are happy with us because we're paying healthy dividends again."

"And your people?" I asked.

"They did it. Once we got our leadership team focused, we marched straight ahead. They engaged our people, but our people did it. They helped us start over. And we made it."

Herbert and his leadership team started over. Their people started over. They connected the dots. They're connected today.

"And as long as I'm here, they'll stay connected," he promised.

NOTE: The story of Dana Herbert and Cosine is adapted from several consulting engagements of which I've been part. I've drawn upon the best of what these leaders did and consolidate it into one story, while preserving the clients' desires for anonymity.

CHAPTER 17

Are You Willing?

*Where the willingness is great, the difficulties
cannot be great.*

— Niccolo Machiavelli, *The Prince*

I hope you've enjoyed this book so far. As you can guess, and as I'm sorry to say, there isn't a simple formula for connecting the dots. Wouldn't it be nice if there were three or four steps to quick success? It would have made writing this book much easier and much faster, too.

But this book tells the truth. There's no quick fix. Connecting the dots is hard work. If it were easy, everybody would have done it by now. Throughout the book, I've tried to emphasize that to create a turned-on, excited, engaged group of people who are passionate about what they do requires the right tools and techniques, the right knowledge and skills, and loads of hard work. Execution is almost everything. Yet behind it all there must be strong, focused leadership. Connecting the dots *starts* with leadership.

You probably consider yourself to be a leader of sorts. Maybe you're even pretty good. Maybe you're one of the best. Maybe you think you have what it takes to be the best. Maybe you think you'd like to make a go of it now. Let's see whether you're ready.

Figures 17-1, 17-2, and 17-3 comprise a questionnaire that we use with business leaders who say they're serious about improving people performance. The questionnaire lists a series of activities that are necessary to connect the dots. It enables a business leader to begin to prioritize what he or she is willing to do and by when. The completed survey questionnaire represents a "Connecting the Dots Commitment Index."

Have a go at it. Complete the questionnaire and check your scores. They'll let you know how committed—how ready you are—to begin the process of generating higher levels of commitment and performance from your people.

Every Person in Our Organization Should...

1. Understand our competitive and economic environment and customer requirements.
   We must begin to do this...
   ❏ Now   ❏ In 6 Months   ❏ In 1 Year   ❏ Don't Do

2. Know how what they do every day relates to company goals and results.
   We must begin to do this...
   ❏ Now   ❏ In 6 Months   ❏ In 1 Year   ❏ Don't Do

3. Contribute to setting performance goals for their area.
   We must begin to do this...
   ❏ Now   ❏ In 6 Months   ❏ In 1 Year   ❏ Don't Do

4. Know how they can influence business decisions.
   We must begin to do this...
   ❏ Now   ❏ In 6 Months   ❏ In 1 Year   ❏ Don't Do

5. Know how to read financial statements, including the balance sheets, income, and cash flow statements.
   We must begin to do this...
   ❏ Now   ❏ In 6 Months   ❏ In 1 Year   ❏ Don't Do

6. Know they'll share in the company's success based on their contributions.
   We must begin to do this...
   ❏ Now   ❏ In 6 Months   ❏ In 1 Year   ❏ Don't Do

7. Participate in regular (at least weekly) meetings focused on improving their business unit, team, or individual performance.
   We must begin to do this...
   ❏ Now   ❏ In 6 Months   ❏ In 1 Year   ❏ Don't Do

Figure 17-1. Readiness questionnaire, part 1—everybody.

you're not ready. In that case, it's okay. It's better to know now than after you've committed yourself to your people. It's better to not say unless you're ready to do.

To both the 80-scorers and under-80-scorers, good luck!

CHAPTER 18

Twenty Things You Can Do Now

Of all the things I've done, the most vital is coordinating the talents of those who work for us and pointing them toward a certain goal.

— Walt Disney, 1954

Y ou say you're willing. Let's get started. Here are 20 specific steps you can take, beginning right now. Choose the order in which you take them based on your company's needs, how connected you are, and your strengths and weaknesses.

1. Get your leadership team together. Share with them what *you* got out of this book and how and where you think it applies to your company. Ask them to read it. Discuss it together. Put a game plan together to connect the dots better than you do now. There is always room to improve the connection. Make a list of your top three priorities for connecting the dots for your people.

2. Create a written communication policy. Keep it simple. Four

words ("Always tell the truth") or four pages. Don't worry about the words. Worry about what they mean. Make sure there's nothing in what you plan to say that you can't or won't do. What information will you share and why? What won't you share and why? What performance sacrifices are we making by not sharing? Remember that there's a correlation between how open you are and how much you value your people. Valuing people is a key principle of companies that connect the dots the best. Identify five things you'll do, starting today, to begin to live the policy.

3. Create a simple Statement of Expectations for Leaders. List five specific roles you and your leadership team will play in getting people connected to your goals and vision. Communicate the statement to everyone in the company who has leadership responsibility. Find someone who's living up to the expectations. Tell them they are. Find someone who isn't. Tell them they're not. Coach them. Encourage them. But let them know that they have no options. If they improve, tell them so. If they don't, tell them. If they can't live up to the expectations, replace them with someone who does.

4. Read your company's goals and business strategy. Can they be explained to the salesperson on the floor, the forklift operator, the receptionist, or the maintenance person on the night shift so that they can relate to them? If not, simplify them. Make them comic book simple.

5. Create the story. It's what you want everybody in the company to understand. If they do, you'll be more apt to win than if they don't. Next to each of the five information categories, write a simple statement. Next to that statement, identify five things you'll begin to do immediately to communicate the story through your actions.

6. Find 10 examples where systems, programs, policies, proce-

dures, or organizational structure send messages that conflict with your story. They're there! Which three are doing the most damage to performance? Create a specific plan to align them with the story. Tell everyone what you did and why.

7. Create a specific plan for the formal communication media. Make sure nothing gets into these channels that doesn't help tell the story. Implement the plan.

8. Ask yourself what program, project, or activity is really important to your ability to win. If you aren't its champion already, become its champion. Spend time on it. Ask people who are working on the effort how they're doing. Ask them what they need to help them make it a success. When it does succeed, make a lot of noise about it. If it doesn't, make a lot of noise about their nice try. Find another high-priority project to champion.

9. Teach one person every day why it's important to connect people and what they do to your goals and vision. Tell that person why it's important and what it takes. Tell her to connect the dots in the story over and over again. When you've said it enough, tell it one more time.

10. Look at what you did last month. What got most of your attention? What got second most? Does your calendar help communicate your story? Adjust next month's calendar to tell the story better than last month's calendar did.

11. At least twice a week, take a trip deep into your company. Listen to people. Ask questions. What's on their minds? What's preventing them from being the best they can be? What are your customers saying about you? Do they understand where you're going? Do they know how what they do links to the company's bigger goals? Do they think they're making a difference? What's in their way? From each trip, list five things you can do differently to better connect people to the com-

pany and its vision and strategy. Act on those five things. Tell people what you did.

12. Find two people out in the company who are helping you tell the story through their actions. Tell them. Tell others you told them. Look for things people are doing that may be countercultural or "against the rules" but critical to telling the story. If you lead a big company, reach way into the organization and find someone to recognize. Call him personally. Write him a note in your own handwriting. That story will be told faster and with more credibility than 100 videos.

13. Perform one symbolic act each month to help communicate the story. Look for seemingly bizarre, slightly out-of-character but credible acts that get people's attention.

14. Make sure every person in your company becomes business literate. Make it a condition of employment. Before anyone can go onto the floor, run a machine, operate a computer, or answer a customer phone call, they need to understand the business of the business. Teach people how to read financial statements. Tell them financial statements are stories about people and what they do. Make sure people understand their place on the financial statements.

15. Begin a regularly scheduled, disciplined cycle of meetings, or huddles, that focus on managing the numbers. The meetings should be on company time. They shouldn't be "extra things we do," but the way the business is run. Use meetings to recognize and celebrate people for living the story. Never cancel one of these meetings because you have other things to do (a higher priority). Personally participate in the meetings.

16. Scrutinize your working environment. Describe your office, store, or plant as if you were visiting it for the first time. Is it alive and electric, or is it tired and asleep? Is it stuffy and formal or light and informal? Does it bring people together or

keep people apart? Find five things you can do now to change your environment to help you tell the story.

17. Create ad hoc rewards and recognition, including small games around achieving small wins. Focus on the things that could get in the way of hitting your big targets.

18. Make sure everyone in the company knows how to solve problems, really knows continuous improvement problem-solving techniques. You can't tell a story about wanting to improve and not give people the basic skills and tools to do so.

19. Actively participate in your company's orientation, training, and development programs. Tell the story each time you do. After people have been with the company three weeks, invite them back together. Ask them where the story is being told, where you can do better. From these meetings, make a list of three ways to better tell the story.

20. If you have a communication function in your company, meet with the people in that function. Tell them to stop doing anything they're doing that doesn't tell the story or measurably improve performance. Tell them you want them to focus at least 80 percent of their time on discovering and removing communication barriers to operating performance.

Now, start with number 1 and do it all over again. And then again. Forever!

Part Five: Lessons Learned

- The process of connecting people to the business strategy, getting everyone on board and moving in the same direction is hard work, but it's doable. In today's competitive world, leaders really have no choice. Having your people and their energy act as a drag on your company's performance doesn't represent a legitimate option.

- Starting over starts with holding a mirror up to yourself. Your own people and your customers often represent the best mirror, although asking them what they think is sometimes painful when you know you aren't going to like the answers. But it's necessary, and in the end you'll be better for it. The fact that you asked them says something about your intentions. And when you act on their responses, you begin to build your credibility and their ownership in what you're trying to accomplish.

- Take a hard look at your leadership team. At first, there may be some visceral believers, a few skeptics, and a resistor or two, like Dale. Help the visceral believers win. Help them be your ambassadors. When the visceral believers do well, reward and recognize them in a way that's visible to the skeptics. Help them cross the goal line. I've seen some resistors eventually turn into visceral believers. I've seen others leave the company voluntarily. The best leaders are patiently impatient with resistors. They give them direction, tell them what they expect of them, give them support, and *hold them accountable*. If you don't hold them accountable, you're communicating that you will sanction their continued resistance. "He's really not serious about what he says," they'll think. That's the *say-do* gap again.

- Create the story. Align everything you say and everything you do with that story.
- Reward, recognize, and celebrate.
- Do it all again and again until you have it down perfect.

PART SIX

The Communication Function

CHAPTER 19

Organizational Communication: A Vision

Our work is the work of the business;
achieving our goals, attaining our vision.
That's it.

— Bob Libbey, Senior Communication
Professional, Communication,
UnumProvident

Most large companies maintain a function devoted to internal or employee communication. The profession's term for this is organizational communication—having to do with managing the communication process inside the organization. Many small companies don't have a function like this.

As far as I've been able to tell, there's no correlation between the presence of an organizational communication function, its size or the number of dollars allocated to it, and communication effectiveness inside the business.

That's because most communication functions aren't really organizational communication functions. They're formal media functions.

To survive, today's communication function must be reinvented. To accomplish this, it needs to operate on the basis of the following four principles.

Assume Strategic and Operational Relevance

The reinvented employee communication function needs to focus on improving business performance by engaging people in the business. It needs to focus less on improving communication for communication's sake, as often is done now, and more on solving specific business problems. It needs to shift from being means- or process-focused to being more ends- and results-focused. It must help the leadership and the people of the organization connect the dots.

It needs to make sure people are focused on the right things, *right* being defined as those critical processes, capabilities, and success factors that are critical to winning. And it needs to focus on getting information to people when they need it in order to make the right decisions on behalf of the team or enterprise.

Linda Baker, a retired vice president of communication at Visa International, was a reinventing pioneer when some of her managers came to her and asked if she'd help them communicate the business strategy to Visa employees. She counseled them to go a step further. Instead of having people attend meetings about a seemingly distant business strategy, she proposed using the strategy communication opportunity to build business literacy. The objective was to enable everyone to see how he or she can make a difference and then provide the information necessary on a regular basis so people can make that difference. The Visa initiative was both strategic and operationally relevant.

Allstate Insurance has identified tight correlations between communication effectiveness; employee satisfaction, retention, and productivity; and customer satisfaction. When employee survey scores increase on four key questions, so does each of the four performance indicators: employee satisfaction, retention, productivity, and customer satisfaction. When the scores go down, so does performance. The four questions relate to being treated with respect and dignity, delivering customer-focused quality, caring about business decisions' effects on customers, and the company's commitment to its customers.

Allstate uses this understanding of what drives results to improve results in key areas of their business.

At Sears, too, is a familiar story by now. The company used business learning—connecting the dots—to help people understand their role in improving the company. An important communication device was a series of six, 4-foot learning maps. On the maps were charts and graphs that were integrated into scenes with familiar images and a very basic story line.

The story line on one of the first learning maps, which was entitled "A New Deal on Retail Street," depicted how the competitive environment has changed since the 1950s. It showed the frequency of consumer trips to shopping malls declined by two-thirds between 1985 and 1995. A key Sears leader explains: "We had a forklift operator who looked at this and said, 'Wait a minute, if people are going to the mall one-third as often, and all our stores are in malls, why are we spending so much money remodeling those stores?' Access to information is what motivates change and improvement."

When Wal-Mart sells a Philips-Magnavox television at one of its stores, the cash register transaction sends a signal to a Philips Electronics plant in Kentucky. That signal communicates the following to a self-directed work team: "We just sold a specific model of a Philips-Magnavox television set. Please build and ship us another one just like it ASAP." The team builds the TV, and within hours it's on a truck en route to the empty shelf at the Wal-Mart store. Managing communication at this speed helps Wal-Mart keep its costs down through low to no inventories.

Managing communication to improve operating performance means moving information at twitch speed so that people have the ability to make the right decisions right now. Twitch speed is whatever the customer says it is. Twitch speed isn't when the next publication deadline rolls around, when we get around to it, or when everybody's had a chance to sign off.

Managing communication to improve operations means using a blend of high tech and high touch. We need to get maximum use from every bit of technology that's available. But we also need to understand that connecting the dots requires appealing to both the head and the heart. Despite all the wonderful technology at our fingertips, people still need to hear the sincerity behind the words: "Job well done," "I care about you," and "How can I help you be your best?"

The new role of the communication function should be to help guide—but not always lead—this process.

Manage Communication for Value

If assuming strategic and operational relevance represents a change in the *kind of work that's performed,* managing employee communication for value represents the return on the investment made in that work.

Business leaders should ask themselves: If the employee communication function ceased operation tomorrow, would the business suffer as a result? That is, if you're a publicly traded company, would the stock price shudder? Would earnings decline? Would customer satisfaction trend downward? Would costs ease upward? Would the new product development and commercialization process become more protracted? Would there be any measurable impact on the business?

Few communication professionals I know believe that important performance indicators would be affected one scintilla if the employee communication function in their organizations closed shop today. Yet every communication professional I know understands that effective and efficient information sharing is required to improve stock price, earnings, customer satisfaction, costs, and new product development.

So if the primary performance measures require superior communication management, yet none would be affected if the employee communication function closed its doors, the employee communication function must be focusing on the wrong things.

Recent research we've conducted indicates that only about 20 percent of the work performed in employee communication functions could, even with a considerable stretch, be referred to as strategic, value-adding work. More than half the work performed in today's employee communication function is devoted to producing or distributing printed or electronic media, getting stuff out the door in accordance with the old, and outmoded, role of the communication function.

The reinvented employee communication function must be a slave to producing a high value-to-cost ratio. That is, for every dollar it spends, it must deliver the largest possible return in terms of things that matter to the business—quality, service, revenues, costs, productivity, etc.

Tom Harris is responsible for internal communication at Toyota's huge Georgetown, Kentucky, plant. His primary focus is to make sure 8000 people in that 8 million square foot plant always have the information they need to improve eight performance indicators related to safety, quality, cost, and production.

"Sure, people need to understand the big picture, what's going on in the global marketplace," Harris says. But within that context, our goal in communication is to make sure every team member knows what's required for Toyota to succeed and how he or she can directly influence success. That's not a one-shot deal. It requires making sure every minute of every day we are getting the right information to the right people so they can make the right decisions about safety, quality, costs, and production. That's a huge communication undertaking in a plant this size. But it's the only way I know of for the communication function to contribute directly to the bottom line… to add value to Toyota."

"Let's face it," says Bob Libbey, one of the country's top communication practitioners, "if your work isn't making for more efficient, effective, and profitable management of your business, your business doesn't need you."

Counseling and Business Partnering

When Ed Robertson, employee communication manager at FedEx, talks about managing communication inside that far-flung corporation of 140,000 people, he talks from an internal consultant's perspective. "I'm convinced that today's emerging workplace issues demand that we [as a profession] get involved in helping others communicate more effectively by facilitating the process of communication inside the organization," he says.

Therefore, Robertson spends much of his time:

- Helping line managers throughout FedEx understand their role in the communication and information-sharing process.
- Assessing and diagnosing, teaching and developing managers' communication competencies.
- Removing barriers that prevent or hinder managers who want to improve their communication skills.
- Providing measurement and rewards to managers for being competent communicators.

"The work isn't easy, and on its face, it's unsettlingly intangible," says Robertson. The prospect of working to help others communicate better through more of a consulting role than we've performed in the past is inviting in terms of the potential it offers, yet it can be terrifying in terms of the additional roles, knowledge, and skills that it requires.

"Let's be honest," he adds, "not everyone in our field welcomes the idea of giving up the comfort that exists in creating a tangible product like a newsletter or a video. But the fact is, many of us are facing daunting communication challenges that are pulling us outside the traditional comfort zone of conventional media-based communication strategies to tackle a different set of communication needs."

John LaForgia and Chris Gadde, top communication practitioners at the Mayo Clinic, have guided the clinic's communication division through the reinvention process. They created a team whose mission it was to develop a specific plan for shifting skills and knowledge away from the traditional media production model to one focused on consulting, business problem-solving, and building stronger internal relationships. There's a true success story and a model for everyone.

As employee communication assumes a role of counseling and partnering with line managers, the work of practitioners will change. They'll spend more time in the field learning the business of the business, from leaders, customers, and other employees. With this knowledge, communication practitioners will focus increasingly on developing plans to help fix real-time business problems.

Here's an example.

A large financial institution was competing against companies that were getting new products and services to market faster than it was. Increasing speed to market is critical to competing successfully in that industry. The employee communication function proposed to line management a way to identify the extent to which ineffective communication was contributing to the speed-to-market problem and then built a plan to eliminate communication as a weakness. The plan in-

cluded removing geographic and functional boundaries to information sharing and introducing new rewards and recognition that sup-
plied the "what's in it for me" for people in research and development. Because the speed-to-market issue was critical to business
success, line management accepted the proposal and implemented the
plan.

As communication practitioners move toward the status of business consultants and make themselves strategically and operationally
relevant in ways that add clear value, they must also adopt one more
principle if their reinvention of the function is to succeed.

Foster Integration and Create Alliances

I'm heartened by the increasing number of communication-related
meetings I have with clients in which multiple disciplines are present.
But there are still far too many instances when I'm called to help
address a communication problem and only the communication function is represented at the meeting. More than one global company
maintains multiple functions assigned the task of improving organizational communication. One, for example, has an internal communication department and another called human resource communication to deal with HR-related issues, such as pay and benefits. But
aren't all internal communication issues HR-related in that they relate
to the people of the organization? How can you disconnect the communication that emanates from performance management systems,
including measurement and rewards, from the rest of the business?
Yet in more than one organization, these two functions never (or refuse
to) talk to one another.

I was working with a company that by its own admission oper-
ated out of organizational silos. We developed a study to identify communication issues that were contributing to a declining trend in key
performance indicators, namely quality, productivity, and cost. Mid-

way through the diagnosis, people from the human resources function called time-out and complained that much of what we were doing in the project was work that should be reserved for the people in human resources. Perhaps. Perhaps not. But after having observed many staff functions playing their age-old turf games, I can tell you what these staff people also seem to understand but won't say openly: petty territoriality drains energy, reduces productivity, and adds cost and time to any improvement effort.

Communication doesn't know functional boundaries. The reinvented communication function must address communication systemically, not functionally. That means including people with knowledge of technology, finance, human resources, training and development, line management, and the legal department in operationally relevant communication discussions, problem-solving, and implementation.

Bob Libbey says that when "strategic communication is done well—when it's managed as deliberately as any of our lines of business—it's really more about management than it is about communication. With the strategic approach, we are helping to run the business better, and in the process, we transcend the artificial boundaries around our function, which in the past have been drawn so brightly by a more functional, tactical approach to communication."

If we decide to build business literacy and create better line of sight between business performance goals and individual contributions toward those goals, we may need to create partnerships with people in finance.

If we need to improve the speed of information delivery to our suppliers, as Wal-Mart did, we may need to form partnerships with the people in technology. The debate I hear regularly over who should have responsibility for intranets, for example, misses the real question entirely. The question should be: Whom do we need in our alliance to build the most value-adding intranet? Then, let's work together to use the intranet to solve real business problems. That's what

Microsoft does. A lot of people loosely and informally contribute to the vast amount of information Microsoft people have access to. It may appear chaotic on the surface, but deep down, it works. Quibbling over domain doesn't add value to the enterprise, and it contributes to lower performance. Customers don't care who does the job.

If we need to improve leadership communication, we need to include people whose expertise lies in organizational and leadership development as well as measurement and accountability systems that emphasize the importance of leadership communication.

Increasingly, it becomes apparent that the organization is best served when all staff functions work out of one home and lines of responsibility or expertise are diminished. The shared-services or corporate services concept being implemented in a lot of organizations today seems to represent the first stage of this journey. Among the many advantages of this approach are that it helps reduce the unproductive departmental and functional quibbling that goes on in so many organizations. It engages people in broader business thinking, as opposed to narrower functional thinking. It provides professional development opportunities by giving people exposure and, in turn, added knowledge and skills in areas of specialty other than their own. The overall business is more apt to benefit through enhanced performance and efficiency.

When we're helping a company reinvent the communication process, business leaders usually say they want more strategic guidance. Communication practitioners say they want to provide more of that counsel. But there's often a disconnect. Business leaders often have difficulty visualizing *their* communication people as the strategists and counselors they're seeking. The communication people have become niched by their history, by the tactical, media-oriented work they've performed in the past. Sometimes the perception is fair, sometimes it's not. Often, communication practitioners don't have the skills and knowledge to provide that strategic guidance. The objective, then, is for the communication people either to demonstrate that they have what it takes to provide solid counsel on major business issues that are on the forefront of the CEO's mind or to build the skills and knowledge they need to perform that role. Unfortunately, too many practitioners erroneously think they have what it takes, try to proffer strategic advice, and only perpetuate their media-oriented image.

To change their perceptions, communication practitioners will have to build skills and knowledge in such disciplines and areas as change management, business economics and business literacy, measurement, knowledge management, internal consulting, globalization, outsourcing, and outsourcing management, among others.

The communication reinvention process is underway. It needs to move faster, and it no doubt will when business leaders and communication practitioners realize that it's possible, that it doesn't have to be threatening, and that it is the best hope for communication professionals to increase their skills and knowledge and their value to their organizations.

In the end, customers and shareholders will be better off.

CHAPTER 20

Reinventing the Communication Function

Corporations must realize that the communication process is a business process vital to success. If we don't manage the business process now, communication will continue to evolve without forethought or evaluation and without adequate return on investment.

— Michael Critelli, CEO, Pitney Bowes

Reinventing the communication function has one overarching goal: to better align the function and what it does to the company's strategic goals.

After a communication function has been reinvented:

- Work performed by the function is better geared to improving company performance.

- There's a better value-to-cost relationship with the work that's performed.
- People in the function are more productive.
- Morale tends to be higher because people are making a greater contribution to the enterprise.
- The skills and knowledge of the people in the function are elevated.

The reinvention process has three steps. During the first step, leadership needs to agree on its communication philosophy (Chapter 10) and on the communication environment that it wants to create. They then need to determine what role, if any, a function should play in helping to create and/or maintain that environment. During the second step, the current function needs to be thoroughly analyzed. And during the third step, the new function must be planned and implemented.

Step 1

During Step 1, the leadership needs to be honest with themselves about what kind of communication environment they want to build to help the business perform better. Chapter 10 is replete with issues that need to be resolved. Then the leaders need to decide what they want the communication function to do. Many CEOs have told me they want a function staffed by strategic, proactive consultants. But strategic proactive consultants have knowledge and skills that come with a price. They also are passionate about being strategic and proactive. They aren't likely to want to get down in the weeds and be your wordsmith artists. They're inclined to push back at you if they think you're moving down the wrong path. They probably won't be as acquiescent as the media-oriented people you've been used to. If you say you want a strategic function and you create a strategic function, yet don't permit them to be strategic, they probably won't hang around for long.

On the other hand, is your real goal to create a function that produces and disseminates communication media, and that does its job economically? If that's your goal, the skills and knowledge of the people within the function will be quite different than the skills and knowledge of strategic consultants. Or do you want a hybrid—a little of both?

There's no right answer. But you need to decide based on what's best for the business, just as you would make similar decisions around other staff and line functions.

Step 2

Assessing the current function should also be as rigorous as it would be for other parts of your business. An assessment should tell you four kinds of information:

- The nature of work performed by the function
- How much it costs to perform the work
- How important and effective the work is
- The current function's capabilities; what they are good at and not good at

In the following pages, I'm going to introduce you to four analytical tools that could help you assess your communication function. Blended with the value-to-cost assessment discussed in Chapter 11, these tools, properly employed, could help you conduct a rigorous analysis that will produce useful decision-making data.

Activity Analysis

An activity analysis identifies what work is performed in the function, who does it, and where, when, and why it's done. To conduct this analysis, members of the communication function complete a written questionnaire that invites them to record how they currently use their time. The activity analysis shows how the people in the function allocate their time across specific communication activities. It categorizes that work by job category and helps identify opportunities for improving the balance between high-value strategic work and lower-value tactical work. Figure 20-1 depicts part of an activity analysis from an electric utility.

Work performed at the top of the pyramid—strategy/planning work—tends to add more value to the enterprise than work at the bottom of the pyramid—administration. However, lower-value work can cost less to perform than strategic work. As you can see, approximately half the work performed by the function is categorized as development/execution work, essentially designing, producing, and disseminating formal communication media. However, the highest paid people inside this communication department, the director, managers, and team leaders, spend only 60 percent of their time on strategic work, meaning essentially that everything these people do before lunch is nonstrategic, relatively lower-value-added work.

Armed with this information, the utility began to redeploy resources so work was better balanced to meet their needs.

How do you shift the work?

Some work can be eliminated. A number of communication practitioners have just stopped doing certain lower-value work. Most people don't even notice that the work has stopped because it wasn't adding value to begin with.

Some work can be outsourced. Motorola was one of the first companies to outsource all of the writing that went into various formal communication media, such as publications. Steve Biederman, the company's employee communication manager, correctly believed that there were many superior sources of writing support available to him, so he went out into the open market and bought writing support just as

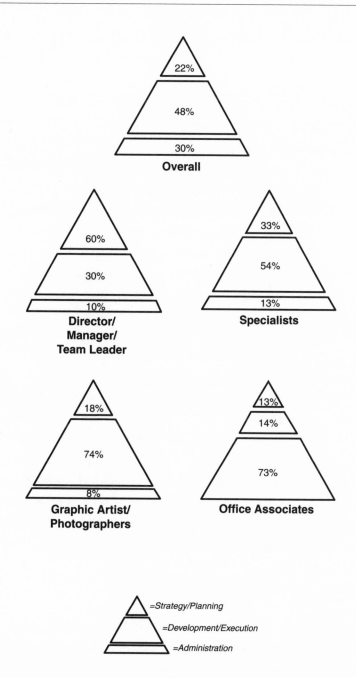

Figure 20-1. Example of an activity analysis summary for an electric power company.

Motorola buys many other services and products. Biederman figured if the company could hire outside legal counsel, engage advertising agencies, and purchase component parts for its various products, and do so in a way that was consistent with the company's Six Sigma quality standard, it could hire writing talent as well. He did and it's been working well for years.

Some work can be more efficiently performed through better use of technology. Many communication functions already have made the switch to Web-based technology as a vehicle for information dissemination. However, as was discussed in Chapter 6, The Power of Huddles and Channels, there's still a lot of work to do to make that information operationally relevant. Nevertheless, technology can help a communication function make the shift to performing higher-value work overall.

Cost Analysis

A cost analysis gives a company information about and develops a detailed understanding of the costs and staff time associated with managing specific communication initiatives and processes. Gathering the cost information is relatively straightforward: What does it cost to do each of the things the function does? The true cost of your investments includes staff salaries and other related expenses, too.

Figure 20-2 shows the overall costs by full-time equivalent employees (FTEs) and by operational costs.

Value-to-Cost Assessment

A value-to-cost assessment provides rich data that helps a leader identify the return the company's getting on specific communication processes, activities programs, or media. It assesses a communication portfolio much as a leader would assess a business portfolio. Using a written survey instrument, it can reveal how important people in your

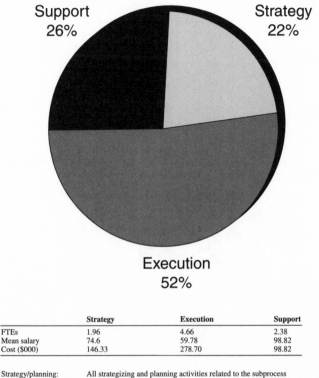

Support
26%

Strategy
22%

Execution
52%

	Strategy	Execution	Support
FTEs	1.96	4.66	2.38
Mean salary	74.6	59.78	98.82
Cost ($000)	146.33	278.70	98.82

Strategy/planning:	All strategizing and planning activities related to the subprocess
Development/execution:	All communication development and execution activities related to the subprocess
Support:	All coordinating, arranging, including typing, filing, and tracking activities related to the subprocess

Figure 20-2.

organization believe specific components of the communication system are to achieving company goals. It reveals how effective those components are. Blended with an analysis of the cost of those components of the system, a leader can determine the value-to-cost of each component.

Figure 20-3 is a chart derived from a value-to-cost assessment at a medical center. The chart represents a baseline. It creates a wealth of data that can be used to redeploy resources to the upper-right quadrant—high importance, high effectiveness—at the least cost.

Most, but not all, initiatives that fall into the lower-left-hand box

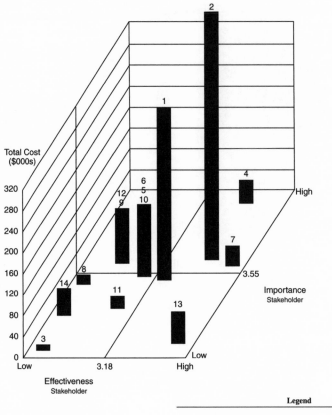

Effectiveness
Stakeholder

Client

Figure 20-3. Employee communication at a hospital.

are flawed in some way. New initiatives that survey respondents have limited exposure to often fall into the lower-left-hand box—low importance, low effectiveness. Setting aside these new and perhaps innovative communication components, everything else in this box is flawed. They should immediately be put on hold until the flaw is found and removed. Otherwise, you're knowingly spending money on a communication activity that consumes resources but isn't improving business performance.

The value-to-cost assessment frees up time and money. In an electric utility of 5000 people, the value-to-cost assessment identified $1.25 million that was being spent on communication activities that were either unimportant or ineffective. Through the cost analysis, it was determined that the equivalent of six people were spending all their time on flawed activities. The company was able to redeploy six people and $1.25 million in a way that added more value.

Another feature of the value-to-cost assessment is that it makes it easy to address so-called sacred cows and pet projects that have existed seemingly forever, despite their failure to contribute to company performance.

Al moved from chief operating officer to chief executive officer of a retail company. When he assumed his new role, he created a publication that he thought would help him communicate his vision and strategy for the company. Al wanted significant control over the publication. He wrote articles for it. He tinkered with it. He edited it. He sent it to his top management team for their reviews. The legal department approved half of each issue's contents. Al took forever to get back to his communication people with the final product. His communication people told him employee reactions to the publication were negative. "Old news," they responded. "Varnished information," they said. "It doesn't reflect reality," they told him.

A value-to-cost assessment confirmed what employees were saying. Al's publication scored in the lower-left quadrant of the grid. It consumed more than $140,000 annually. When Al got the data, he quickly killed the publication as it existed and replaced it with one that was more substantial, more timely, and more reality-based. Figure 20-4 captures it graphically.

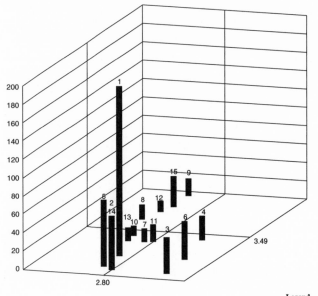

Legend

	Process		Comm. Total Cost ($000s)
1	1.1	Employee Publication	xxx.x
2	1.2	Other Newsletters	xx.x
3	1.3	News Clippings	xx.x
4	1.4	Bulletin Board Materials	xx.x
5	1.5	Videos	xx.x
6	1.6	Electronic Communication	xx.x
7	1.7	Employee Special Events	xx.x
8	1.8	Employee Feedback Systems	xx.x
9	1.9	Employee Education/Training	xx.x
10	1.10	Employee Recognition Communication	xx.x
11	1.11	Initiative Specific Communication	xx.x
12	1.12	Senior Management and Employee Meetings	xx.x
13	1.13	Interactive Voice Response System	xx.x
14	1.14	Consulting and Counseling	x.x
15	1.15	Senior Management Communication	xx.x

Scales

Importance	Effectiveness
1 - Not important	1 - Does not meet expectations
2 - Somewhat important	2 - Meets some expectations
3 - Important	3 - Meets majority of expectations
4 - Very important	4 - Meets all expectations
5 - Critical	5 - Exceeds expectations

Figure 20-4. Internal communication.

Part Six: Lessons Learned

- Communication functions in most companies today aren't really communication functions. They devote most of their time and attention only to the formal communication media and channels.

- Most communication functions in companies were designed for a time that no longer exists. They need to reinvent themselves. They need to assume more strategic and operational relevance. They need to manage communication for value. They need to become counselors and business partners. They need to align and integrate with other key staff functions and line operations.

- The organization's leadership must decide what kind of communication environment is required in order to win in the marketplace. They need to determine the function's role in creating and fostering that environment. The function must undergo a rigorous analysis. Resources then need to be redeployed to create maximum value-to-cost.

Epilogue

All of the assets in your organization are inert until someone does something with them. People will do the right things with those assets when they're informed, involved, and understand that it's in their best interest to help the team win. This is called connecting the dots. It links people and what they do to the organization's vision and strategy.

Business leaders who want to win are working hard to connect the dots. It is hard work. There's no book or formula that will guarantee success at connecting the dots. I've been in business too long and witnessed too many successes and failures to know that connecting A to B to C will not always lead to D. Today's business environment is too turbulent and there are too many variables to be able to ensure that you will be able to connect the dots, even after reading this book. But I will assure you that the principles, processes, tools, and techniques explored in this book have been used by others to successfully connect the dots.

Connecting the dots pays off. It focuses energy. It creates excitement and passion. It delivers hard, cold business results.

In this increasingly competitive, speed-driven, technology-oriented world, winners increasingly will be distinguished by their ability to connect the dots, to get everyone in their organizations moving together toward a common purpose.

The ability to connect the dots will be a critical capability for any organization. It will give anyone who does it well a source of competitive advantage. The numbers argue the case. It makes common sense. And you can do it.